When Women Talk

EMPOWERING EACH OTHER
ONE STORY AT A TIME

When Women Talk

EMPOWERING EACH OTHER
ONE STORY AT A TIME

COMPILED BY

BRIGITTE LESSARD-DEYELL

Published By

WOMEN TALK
Women Sharing Stories

Women Talk
208 Covepark Rise NE Calgary AB T3K 6G3
info@womentalk.ca

Christine Bode and Dawn James, editors
Debra Bernier, cover sculptor
David Moratto, cover and interior book designer

Printed in Canada.

ISBN 978-0-9958337-0-8 (Paperback)
ISBN 978-0-9958337-2-2 (ePDF)
ISBN 978-0-9958337-1-5 (ePUB)

Note to the reader: This book is not intended to dispense psychological
or therapeutic advice. The information is provided for educational and
inspirational purposes only. In the event, you use any of the information
in this book for yourself, which is your constitutional right, the author and
publisher assumes no responsibility for your actions. In some chapters,
names and locations have been changed to protect privacy.

*To all the women who hold a safe space for us
to share our stories and allow us to
talk for those who are silenced.*

*To my wife and my daughter,
may these stories inspire you.
To my son and any man who knows,
loves, and lives with women.*

Contents

The Power of Feminine Energy

By Brigitte Lessard-Deyell

Women Talk was a vision that woke me up at 2 am one morning, and despite not fully understanding what it meant at the time, it was crystal clear to me that I needed to act on this train of thought immediately. I knew that Women Talk was important.

WOMEN TALK EVENTS are held across Alberta and BC where women get together in a space filled with feminine power and energy, where they are allowed to freely share their stories with each other. Women can be shy, timid, and careful when sharing emotional experiences. They must be surrounded with feminine energy and love to feel safe. At Women Talk, we hold such a space for each other. This sisterhood offers a sacred platform that is noticeably empowering to every female in the room. The power of the Divine Feminine is palpable at every Women Talk event in every location. It is beautiful, soft, patient, intuitive, and receptive. Women share emotional, personal stories, often for the first time. No one is superior to anyone else. Everyone's uniqueness is celebrated.

I believe we need more Feminine Energy in the world and the world needs more Women Talk.

In the first 40 years of my life I mostly lived in my masculine energy. I was a tomboy, always gravitating to "boy stuff." I loved all the physical experiences of competitive sports and loved the dominant energy. Although surrounded by women at work, at play, and at home, I was living in my masculine energy. And it served me well.

Then at the age of 41, I became a mother. Motherhood is the most powerful, beautiful energy one can experience. Absolute pure love blossomed in my chest and I can only describe it as the Divine Feminine. However, I started feeling unbalanced. Being a stay-at-home mom doing "mom stuff" was forcing me to live in my feminine energy. Little did I know that an epic internal battle was about to occur.

In its own right Women Talk propelled me into a journey of spiritual awakening. While my head, the masculine side of me, tried to fight back all of the "woo woo stuff" that surrounded me at the Women Talk monthly events, I secretly knew what energy would win that battle. Now that I was a mom, and that part of me was fully awakened, my heart was crying for more. I needed to live my life from a deeper place, a heart-centred place. Surrounded by women who live in that world, my journey began. Meditation, Sisterhood, Sacred Gifts, Angels and so much more. It was, and still is at times, a completely new, strange world.

My Sacred Gifts teacher told me that I would become a "bridge." At the time, I had no idea what that meant, but now I see it. A bridge from a place of common sense to one of spirituality, from our heads to our hearts. I soon came to embrace the fact that my gift is to bridge the gap between the masculine and the feminine.

Once during a guided meditation, I fully experienced the two energies at war. Looking for inspiration to write one of my talks, I decided to meditate. As I sat quietly by my fireplace, feeling warm, relaxed and alone, I picked a guided meditation. The guide asked me to listen to my heart. What was it saying? My marriage immediately came to mind. I could feel its intense love and then I heard my head arguing with my heart. It started listing all that was wrong in my relationship. Then right at that moment the guide softly said, "Don't be surprised if your head is giving you a completely opposite message." I was shocked! How did she know? She knew because we are all composed of masculine and feminine energy and we all choose which side we will listen to and live in.

Gender is an illusion. Masculine and feminine are opposite: left brain vs right brain, straight vs curvy, hierarchical vs cooperative. We are all composed of both, despite the body parts we are born with. Women usually have a higher feminine energy and men usually have a higher masculine energy. Both are necessary to be balanced. The world also needs both for function and beauty.

Many people feel that humanity is in dire need of a return to feminine energy, an energy that has been suppressed for centuries and has been made to feel like the weaker of the two energies. Feminine energy is extremely powerful and is more accepting, inclusive, and peaceful. It is time for women to stand strong and once again speak from their power!

Women living in their feminine energy have been made to feel inferior to men. Over time, women have believed that in order to be successful, they must live in their masculine energy. Today, however, women are rebelling against this long-held misconception as they realize that thinking and living in masculine energy does not work for them. Women are feeling, nurturing creatures meant to experience life in a heart-centered way, with compassion and love.

That balance is also needed in men. Men have been taught to suppress their feminine energy. A man possessing a dominant female energy is ridiculed, treated as weak and un-manly. But when men are forced to live solely in their masculine energy, to the point where they end up "hyper-masculine," violence is often the outcome, in their relationships and in the world.

At a very young age, I was at the receiving end of this "hyper-masculinity" and know how terrifying it can be.

Aboriginal cultures throughout history were matriarchal societies and their peoples understood the significance of living in a more heart-centered, gentle place. They also respected those who had the ability, or gift, of being able to flow from the masculine to the feminine and back again. Gay people in aboriginal cultures were considered to be "Two-Spirited" and were celebrated and respected. Two-Spirited individuals, it was believed, understood and could move fluidly between both the masculine and feminine energies, and were often revered as healers or spiritual leaders.

The Masculine Energy is about power, logic, competitiveness, assertiveness, and rigidity. The Feminine Energy is vulnerable, cooperative, creative, nurturing, receptive, and fluid. I love both and can flow from one to the other depending on the circumstances. I use my masculine energy to attack my goals and achieve desired outcomes. But I love, and more often choose, to live in my feminine energy. Being able to move effortlessly between both energies has truly been a gift for me, and it has helped me understand both powers.

I am just as comfortable playing hockey as I am cooking in the kitchen. I am a fierce, physical competitor and a soft, nurturing mother. I enjoy living with both energies. It is not about balance as much as it is about being able to flow from one energy to the other. I am free to choose which energy I live in, and when. I can fully experience, feel, and live in both energies as I please, but the Divine Feminine Energy is the one I admire now most and the one I prefer to be surrounded by.

Understanding and living in both energies, accompanied by my visionary gift, has prepared me for an extraordinary path. I intend to help my community to raise and celebrate feminine energy. This is my legacy, my small contribution to the world, my life's passion. I want to raise feminine energy in order to make people appreciate all its qualities and Women Talk is my vehicle. It is a beautiful, harmonious place where you can feel the unconditional love of the powerful feminine energy. Together, we help women reach their full potential. Together, we celebrate their uniqueness.

We acknowledge each other's issues and weaknesses and provide healing for our dysfunction. You can feel the honouring of each woman's story. That honour is palpable. As a group, and as individuals, we see each other from our heart-centered space and feel our interconnectedness. At Women Talk you are simply part of the *tribe*. In our collective state, we can heal each other and our communities. We might be a very small pebble in a very large pond, but our ripples are far reaching.

It is my personal belief that by sharing our lessons and teachings, we can create symbiotic energy together that will benefit both men and women and society as a whole. We will share the message of feminine energy that art, music, aesthetics, and love are as important as economics. Together we can raise feminine energy in our cities, our countries and around the world. In the future, perhaps, we can leave war and aggression behind and become a more peaceful society consumed with making the world a better place.

My philosophy behind Women Talk is just that — by sharing their stories, women will make their communities stronger.

ABOUT BRIGITTE LESSARD-DEYELL

Married, mother of two, entrepreneur, and visionary, Brigitte has spent most of her life supporting and empowering women through numerous female-based businesses.

Born a self-confident extrovert, Brigitte learned that sharing her energy to empower other women was something she adored doing. The first part of her life was all about sports, where she learned many of her leadership skills and how to motivate other women to push past their limiting beliefs. That's also where she learned that together we are stronger.

Her insatiable curiosity has led her on the path of a serial entrepreneur. Over the years, she has owned multiple female-based businesses including a women's sports store, a women's gym, a physiotherapy clinic, and a women's trade show, just to name a few! She presently owns Sportsbras.ca and Women Talk and is a professional public speaker. Brigitte is also a Certified Sacred Gifts Guide and has studied and practiced the Law of Attraction's principles for almost 20 years.

Whether it's at the microphone or on camera, you will instantly be moved by Brigitte's larger than life energy. Her "joie de vivre" is contagious. As a motivational speaker, Brigitte inspires women to celebrate their feminine energy, to speak their truth, and stand fully in their power.

Passionate about women having the opportunity to share their stories in a positive, uplifting, safe environment, Brigitte became a story activist and created Women Talk — a monthly event which is spreading to many cities across Canada. Using her Gift of Cultural Integration, she brings together women from all social classes, religions, sexual orientations, and races, and encourages them to respect and celebrate their differences. Women Talk is ordinary women sharing their extraordinary stories.

Brigitte firmly believes that "By Sharing Their Story, Women Make Their Communities Stronger."

www.womentalk.ca
www.sportsbras.ca
www.facebook.com/BrigitteKLessardDeyell
www.linkedin.com/in/brigittelessard-deyell

Ruby Slippers

BY SHARON RENNECKE

Sharon is like an enchantress. When she starts talking, we are all pulled in by her charisma. We sit there, enthralled by her brilliant stories, wondering what the lesson will be. Her metaphors are dazzling and her divine feminine is powerful. Watching this heroine walk a mile in her powerful red ruby shoes is mesmerizing. Her yellow brick road is an inspiration to many.

Brigitte

"You had the power all along my dear"
— GLINDA THE GOOD WITCH

WHY IS IT that we women think our power lies outside of our amazing selves? That in order to be the highest version of ourselves, a metaphorical wand must be waved or a pair of imaginary red glittering heels clicked together three times? Believing you are your own Glinda the Good Witch is an overwhelming thought, and stepping into her shoes is a daunting task.

Are we not the heroines of our own lives? The designers of our destiny? And as such, what is the payoff if we keep waiting for some magical occurrence to propel us to magnificence?

I read a book once where the writer said he would get up each morning, put on his lucky watch, get dressed, fill his lucky coffee cup, and sit down to work on his writing. It occurred to me a week later as I was schlepping about the house in sweats and slippers, completely avoiding my office, that *maybe* he was onto something. I puttered about all morning doing dishes, laundry, and opening mail, basically anything that could keep me in a justifiable state of resistance toward working on my notes for a speaking engagement that evening.

Later that afternoon as I began to get ready, I struggled to muster up the gumption to get in "the zone." As I was expected later that evening to give a motivational talk to a group of women, I felt that a little excitement or enthusiasm might come in handy. However, as I went through the motions, I made a mental list. Shower — check. Hair — check. Face — check. New power dress — check, check! My enthusiasm level, however, remained a gloomy zero on the shiniest self scale.

Put on the shoes... put on the shoes... a little voice kept saying from somewhere in the part of my brain where my inspired self was on hiatus. Put on those four-inch heels and power up! Common sense self said, "Don't be ridiculous, you can't walk in those in the house!" But inspired self prevailed knowing the magnitude of the situation, and so I stepped into a pair of four-inch white strappy platform heels. They were my favorite and they were fabulous!

Bam! Just like that I was taller, and not just in physical height, but taller in presence, in stature, in gumption. Instantly I was a speaker and a motivator again. I was inspiring, I was someone I would want to get to know! I felt like a million bucks, baby! Yeah, best shoes ever!

As I drove the hour-long drive to the venue, I thought about the power of the shoes and it occurred to me that they were much like Dorothy's ruby shoes in The Wizard of Oz. For her the shoes held the power to return her to her beloved home, or so she thought. It was really Dorothy herself who held that power all along, if only she believed she was the heroine of her own life. The good witch Glinda was merely a motivational coach along the way while the hard stuff was all on Dorothy.

Now I realized that my pretty white platforms didn't actually have magical powers but what they did have was the power to push me into manifesting the person I truly was, and needed to step into being, for the occasion at hand. Those shoes were the catalyst for my transforming from comfortably resistant, into daring to shine.

Comfort breeds comfort. For years I held a romantic notion of being a weekend, world-changing warrior with a mug of coffee in my hand, while wearing fuzzy attire and reading socks on my feet. Yep, that's right, reading socks... long, soft, feminine socks dreamt up by some overpaid marketing guru that retailed for $35 at Chapters. In reality, my $5 socks were old and fuzzy from years of washing. Armed with my favourite mug, I would head to the armchair in my office (not the desk) with grand plans to change hearts, inspire minds, and propel women forward into the shiniest versions of themselves, essentially all done in my pj's. I will let you guess how that worked for me and women everywhere... You got it! Inspired to do the work — nope, take a nap — you bet! Leave the work on the chair to bake a batch of warm cookies to round out my comfort party? Mmmm yes, please! Now don't get me wrong, many inspired ideas, processes, and results have come from just such cozy settings. However, "my process" for creating change in my life and the lives of women the world over was cloaked in comfort (aka: resistance), much like the place I was in in my own life. Change requires work, hard work. Uncomfortable work and in four-inch heels! Work that needs more than fuzzy pink socks to pack any sort of punch. There's a reason designers call it the *Power Suit,* ladies!

I am well aware of what does not work for me when my highest self is being called up. I am also well aware of what I need to do to meet myself halfway. Before stepping into the shoes, the suit, the dress, I have to have at least one shred of belief in myself. That's it, just a smidge of belief that what I have to say is important — that it might be important to someone else's journey. I have to believe in my purpose, and with a mighty shove propel myself into my own light. Every woman's journey is unique, and for some the belief may lie in putting that first brush stroke to canvas, it may be signing the offer on her first home, or going back to school after raising her babies. In order to do anything at all we must, like Dorothy, realize that the power lies within; that the belief in ourselves and our personal power is paramount to fulfilling and living the life of our dreams.

So how to find that belief? The meaning behind the meaning of what we love and were born to do? Being passionate about something doesn't necessarily mean we do something about it or with it. Some call it finding your "why". I call it refusing to sit one more day living an unfulfilled and inauthentic life, cloaked in fear, doubt, and crippling inactivity! Sound familiar? Armed with Glinda style quotes, I decidedly show up and wade into my juiciest dreams and shiniest visions, repeating: "Eat the frog." "Who does it serve when you play small?" "What is it going to take to fall madly in love with your life?" These are just a few of my own heel clickers designed to continually remind me of what's at stake here. They remind me that I am worthy of a big, fulfilling life, and that my voice deserves to be heard.

Doesn't it all come down to worthiness? Believing in oneself means believing I am worth it. I am worth all the great things and experiences the universe is conspiring to put on my course — my yellow brick road. I am worth doing the work, worth risking failure and detours and discomfort many times over to get to my Oz. There is no shame in living an uninspired life, it's just that I know better and when we know better, we do better. And really, why live uninspired? Do we not each have a responsibility to show up and shine in our own lives, automatically radiating our light, joy, and fearlessness, to others, and inspiring them to do the same?

I believe every woman has that proverbial pair of ruby shoes. Maybe its a lucky watch, a mug, that one stunning pair of shoes, or whatever item it takes for the spark of belief to be ignited enough for her to get up, dress up, and show up for her one precious life in all her magnificence.

What will it take for you to step into *your* Ruby Slippers?

ABOUT SHARON RENNECKE

Sharon Rennecke is a dynamic speaker and motivator, leading and inspiring women to step into their shiniest selves and live their biggest lives. She is the founder of a life coaching company called 'Dare to Shine'. She believes we all have our own answers within and that once we get past our fear of really seeing ourselves that those answers will come forth to propel us into the grandest, bravest versions of ourselves.

Since her start in women's fitness coaching, she has been coaching and leading women since 2008. She has been a volunteer life coach for Choices International Programs since 2011. In 2012, she completed her formal life coaching through The Coaches Training Institute in California.

Sharon lives in Central Alberta on 20 acres that is her ever evolving canvas, and soul's safe haven. She shares this calming space with a variety of rescued cats, some part time cows, or horses, and her beloved black lab "Moe."

www.sharonrennecke.com
www.facebook.com/sharon.rennecke

I Am Finally Free

By Brenda Hammon

Determined to hear the birds again, Brenda's journey to healing from sexual abuse, rape and attempted murder, is very moving. I find it hard to believe that this strong, well-spoken lady has suffered so much. She is a wealth of information for so many who have suffered and her books and talks help many.

Brigitte

My LIFE-ALTERING JOURNEY began when I was five years old. The things that happened to me at that time would change me and my world forever. No longer was I a carefree little girl, no longer was I innocent of the ways of people, and no longer could I look to my family and friends of my family for comfort and safety.

Throughout my childhood, my adolescence, and into adulthood, my past haunted me. No matter how hard I tried to shove the memories back into the recesses of my brain and forget them, they would eventually come bubbling to the surface. These memories were like a balloon filled with air and forced under water until it eventually escapes your grasp and springs to the surface with such force that it bursts above the water. Such was my life. Without any warning, those haunting memories would break the surface and cause more chaos.

In the beginning of my therapy, I remembered the farm hand's sexual and mental abuse, but I had blocked out the rape done to me by a family member. This hidden memory was the most damning. My only way to escape from my home and the people who had violated my trust was to catch my horse, jump on bareback, and ride away as fast and as far as I could. My horse became my savior and my best friend. I cried on her and I prayed on her for God to take me away from all the pain.

All my decisions were rooted around the abuse and how I viewed myself, the world, and the people that were around me. I trusted no one! My survival depended solely on me.

My first marriage to Alfred was a disaster. Even my choice of wedding dress reflected my childhood abuse. All that was visible was my face and hands. If you coloured my dress black, it looked like a funeral shroud with a vampire cape (minus the high collar). To me, that was the dress I deserved because I felt ugly and needed a dress to match my feelings.

Alfred was an emotional and mentally cruel husband that had a sex obsession that drove him over the edge and ultimately to his death. During our marriage his constant cheating with other women and lying and pure lack of regard for his children had damaged our marriage beyond repair. His possessiveness and jealousy was out of control and got to the point where I was not allowed to talk to anyone, especially a male. When someone talked to me that he didn't approve of, it would be days of the silent treatment then and the accusations would start. Alfred would accuse me of doing what he was doing and thought I was lying about it. It was an emotional roller-coaster and there was just no winning with him.

After 21 years in this emotionally and mentally abusive marriage, I finally managed to leave. I thought I was finally free to have a life that I wanted but that was not to be. Alfred was not the leaving kind. He was jealous and possessive and I was his property. He decided that if he couldn't control me and contain me, then I must die. He threatened me and stalked me during our separation and after we divorced. I was forced to give up my apartment and live on the run. The only contact my daughters and parents had for me was my cell phone number.

During our separation, Bud entered my life, and I believe with all my heart that if it wasn't for him shielding me from Alfred, I wouldn't be here today. During one of my many lawyer visits for the divorce, my lawyer told Bud to never leave my side, for if he did Alfred would kill me. Realistically, Bud couldn't always be there, so I was forced to live in my horse trailer or my car to keep safe from Alfred's reach. This had been a recurring life pattern from childhood: to run, run hard and fast to escape the pain and turmoil, and to escape my life.

Alfred died 18 months after our divorce. With his death came a variety of emotions — guilt being one — as his family blamed me for his death. I also felt shame and relief. Now that Alfred was dead I thought that I could finally have a normal life, but that dream was soon shattered when the RCMP informed me that Alfred had hired someone to kill me. For the next six months I lived in fear that I was going to be shot. When the RCMP finally called our daughters and told them that the investigation into their father's death was over, I figured that they must have found out who he had hired to kill me. The RCMP refused to tell me anything about the investigation as I was not the next of kin. I was totally in the dark. Talking to my daughters about it was out of the question as they were having difficulty dealing with his untimely death and the chaos it had caused for his family. My life couldn't get any worse.

Within weeks of Alfred's death, weird things started to happen to me. I could feel a presence around me that I didn't understand. Suddenly, I saw Alfred standing at the foot of my bed at night. When I refused to allow my mind to accept this, the bed would start shaking, forcing me to put one foot on the floor to stop it.

It was New Year's Eve and Bud and I were sitting by the fireplace. I had closed my eyes and when I opened them I saw Alfred's face staring back at me instead of Bud's. To say that I was freaked out was an understatement. I quickly shut my eyes and opened them again, only to see Bud looking back at me with a puzzled look on his face. I never told him what I had seen. I honestly thought that I was going crazy. Was guilt and shame about Alfred's death reaching out, grasping at my soul, trying to suck me down to hell with him?

The feelings I was experiencing became unbearable and I decided to speak with my new doctor about how Alfred's death was affecting me. I feared my doctor would have me committed to a 'nut house' but instead she referred me to a grief counsellor named Lorraine. That is when my world began to change.

Lorraine was the answer to all my prayers. She unlocked my Pandora's Box and pulled and dragged those long-buried memories to the surface. At times, I felt that I hated her for prying, yet at other times I loved her for helping me.

Throughout my four years of grief counselling with Lorraine, I worked on exorcising the demons of my past. There were times that I couldn't deal with all the memories and the suffocating pain. I would fall into my old habit of running hard and fast once again, until I couldn't go any faster and would eventually have to go back to Lorraine and continue this horrible journey of acknowledging and accepting the truth about my abusers.

I hit the wall three years into the grief counselling therapy when I finally had to accept what my family member had done to me. When I realized that someone else in my family knew what happened and never told anyone until over four decades later, it shook me to my core and literally knocked me off my feet. All those years I had refused to believe the truth: that the haunting images that constantly bubbled to the surface of my conscious mind that felt like sharp arrows piercing me and making me bleed, were in fact real. That was the hardest thing I ever had to face. It took another year to work through that, but in the end I realized that if I wanted to have a 'normal life' (and I had no idea what that looked like) I was going to have to see this through.

I was determined that I was going to deal with all the demons of my past. I made a commitment to conquer them, to leave them in the dust of my tracks and walk away.

After Lorraine and I finished our journey together, I thought, "Wow, I made it! I am finally free from my past!" No longer were those dark shadows hovering over me. My mind was free.

However, although my mind was free, I could still feel Alfred's unsettled presence around me. Fortunately, I met Mary and she introduced me to Hypnotherapy. This therapy enabled me to break all ties with Alfred and stop the feelings of being attacked by him, even though he had not crossed over when he died. It wasn't an easy task but in the end I succeeded.

When I started to write my first book, the five-year-old little girl in me was screaming loud and clear that she wanted to be released from her prison. She wanted me to write her story through *her eyes*, and so my book, "*I can't hear the birds anymore*" was born. During this time, I realized that although my mind was clear and free, my body was not. It wasn't long before my body had to fight infections and strange aliments.

The stress that I had endured for four decades was once again manifesting itself in my physical body.

I was feeling frustrated and angry with my body for continuing to hold onto the past and I wondered how I would ever put those memories behind me. That is when Thrya entered my life and my 'cellular release therapy' began. We worked on releasing all the emotions that were trapped in my cells so that my body was no longer reacting to the dramatic events of the past.

Once my cells were free from trapped emotions, my second book, "*I AM*" sprung forth like a Phoenix from the ashes. I was finally able to tell my story, unencumbered by the past and the aliments that created my turmoil.

After five decades, I am proud to say that my body no longer holds the emotions of my past. My mind is clear and free and I am living the life I was meant to live. I have finally found happiness.

Today, I am neither a victim nor a survivor, but an ordinary woman who is well-adjusted despite my past.

ABOUT BRENDA HAMMON

Brenda and her husband own a Lifestyle Protection Insurance Business, called Spirit Creek Financial, where they provide life, mortgage, disability and group benefits. Brenda also sits on the Advisory Board of one of Canada's' Leading Lifestyle Providers, The Edge Benefits, has competed on the National Circuit in Dressage, and is an international bestselling author.

Her first book, "*I can't hear the birds anymore*" is narrated from a child's point of view and reveals how being sexually molested and raped at the age of five years old affected her life. Proceeds from the sale of this book are used to purchase more books that are donated to women's shelters.

Brenda's sequel book, *I AM*, is told from a woman's perspective. Its story takes readers on the journey of Brenda's life, complete with its triumphs and failures, and shares her determination, resilience, and conviction that there is a better life out there waiting for all of us.

www.spiritcreekpublishing.com
www.brendahammon.com
www.facebook.com/brenda.hammon.9
www.thereishappinessafter.com

Be the Best Version of You!

BY DR. MYLÈNE HOPF

Dr. Hopf is a perfect example of why I think Millennials get a bad rap. She is part of a new breed of doctors who are connected to their clients and communities. Mylene was part of my very first team who founded Women Talk in 2011. She truly believes in supporting her community and sharing her gifts. Her positive attitude is such a pleasure to be around. With her, the future of our world is in good hands.

Brigitte

I HAVE A problem with what people think of me. Or rather, I have a problem with what I think people think of me. This is not a new issue for me, but it is one that became very problematic when it interfered with my ability to provide the absolute best care to one of my patients.

Let me take you back a few years ago, so that this story makes a bit more sense. I've been very blessed in my life to come from a very loving, supportive, privileged family. Not that my parents were excessively wealthy, but I never wanted for food, shelter or love. I was a fairly bright student, athletic, and popular growing up. I didn't worry about grades. I played high-level competitive sports and started working part-time when I was 14. I was fortunate enough to buy my own car when I turned 16 and gained comfortable independence to lead an active social life in high school. Surprisingly, with all my privilege growing up, I never developed a very solid sense of confidence and self-worth. Maybe it's because I always assumed that people would think I was less of a great person if I didn't have myself completely put together 100% of the time. I was so uncomfortable with not being the best at things, whether it was being at the top of my class, or being the captain of the volleyball team, and with keeping up the *appearance* that I had no worries. This followed me into grad school, when I moved to California when I was 21 to begin chiropractic school. I felt so uncomfortable if someone knew something that I didn't, or if someone was discussing a topic that I didn't quite understand or have any working knowledge of. It wasn't reasonable to me that I couldn't possibly know everything about everything, and that asking when I didn't understand would certainly not make me look like a bumbling, incompetent idiot. If I found myself struggling with any area of my studies or training, I would do my best to avoid spending time on them. Looking back now, it seems ridiculous and very counter-intuitive, but I felt as though if everyone *perceived* that I was competent and had all my ducks in a row, this was more important than me *actually* being competent and having all my ducks in a row.

The same strange mentality followed me into my chiropractic practice. I struggled with not knowing the answer to every single question someone would have, or having a conversation with colleagues and not quite following along, but being too embarrassed to pause and clarify, as though it would make me appear unworthy of the degrees on my wall and the Dr. in front of my name. It wasn't as though I knew nothing about what I was doing, don't get me wrong. I was, and am, very good at taking care of my patients. I am decisive and assertive with the care I provide. However, if I had a particularly challenging case, I was hesitant to openly chat with my colleagues for fear that I would look incompetent. I would remain silent even if it meant that the patient might potentially get a more exceptional result. If I made a mistake, it would be disastrous and make my colleagues and patients think so much less of me. And all of this came down to the fact that I was always worried about what I thought people were thinking about me.

Often in life, there comes a turning point, an "ah-ha" moment so to speak. I had a young patient come in to see me. He had been a long-time patient, as was the rest of his family. His mom brought him in because he had fallen at school a couple of weeks prior, knocked his head and been diagnosed with a concussion. He was still suffering from headaches, irritability and neck pain and wasn't recovering well, so his mom wanted me to have a look and get some direction for what needed to happen next. I thought to myself, my goodness, I don't even know what to answer here. I was actually stunned that I had no idea how to properly manage a concussion. In all the hours of study, diagnosis classes, physiology, anatomy and neurobiology that I had taken, I did not have a clear understanding of what needed to happen beyond telling her to let him rest and take it easy for a few days and that it should settle down after that. At that moment, I realized that if I did not tell this patient that I am not the expert to speak with in this situation, this little boy was not going to get the help he needed and he might suffer at the expense of my pride! This was simply unacceptable.

This was my epiphany. It turned my life right around, both professionally and personally. It created urgency in me to do whatever I needed to do to understand this injury. I wanted to be prepared so that the next time someone walked through my doors and had a concussion, I knew with confidence exactly what they needed to do, and that my office was truly the best place for them to be. I practice in a particular area called upper-cervical chiropractic (NUCCA more specifically) and it is meticulously focused on correcting injuries, imbalances and misalignments of the head and neck. Concussions are an injury that chiropractors are confronted with regularly. In essence, you cannot sustain a concussion without an injury to the neck, so the fact that I knew virtually nothing about this injury was abominable to me. The next year, I set out to learn everything I could and speak to everyone I could find that knew more about concussions than I did. I came to the realizaton that I did not feel foolish or inferior to the people I was talking to, in fact I felt empowered and excited. My discussions gave me the opportunity to also fill in gaps in the knowledge of people who didn't know what I knew. And now, I know a lot more than I knew but I know my journey isn't over. In order to truly provide the best, most exceptional care to my patients, I know that I can't just keep up appearances. I can't ride on the coattails of other practitioners in my profession. I need to continuously and consistently learn, question, investigate and desire more. Just because I have a degree and a license to practice does not mean that I don't need to continue to grow. My playing small does not help bring health to a larger community. This is a quote from Marianne Williamson that I've heard many times before, but I now believe I understand the essence of the words:

"Our deepest fear is not that we are inadequate. Our deepest fear is that we are powerful beyond measure. It is our light, not our darkness that most frightens us. We ask ourselves, who am I to be brilliant, gorgeous, talented, and fabulous? Actually, who are you not to be? Your playing small does not serve the world."

I realized that trying to pretend that I was the smartest all the time and not acknowledging that there are many things that I don't know was doing a terrible disservice to my practice, and as a result also to the rest of the world. Having a thirst to grow, to be better, to know more, only allows me to serve and help a greater part of my community, which in turn helps spread ripples throughout even more of the community. There is a saying that you never know how what you say, think, or do today may affect the lives of millions tomorrow, and I believe this is true of every single one of us. You never know if smiling at a stranger instead of just looking down at your phone might be the tipping point for their day. We each have the ability to change the world around us, and I now know that salvaging my pride is not the way to do this. For many years I had confused what other people *perceived* of me as my actual self-worth, and I believe this lessened my ability to contribute even greater things to the world around me.

In closing, I want you to know that you are a gift to the world around you. You become the best version of you when you have a desire to grow, to expand into spaces that you aren't comfortable with and to be okay with not having everything figured out. Your desire to grow creates the ability for you to become an even more amazing, successful person who can then contribute an even greater presence to everyone you meet. So be comfortable being uncomfortable. The only way to grow is to recognize that you don't need to have it all together now. Everybody is on their own journey. Everybody is having their own experience, so don't worry about what you *think* people think of you. What people think of you is none of your business anyway, but when that interferes with your ability to be the best version of yourself, it becomes a much more ominous threat.

ABOUT DR. MYLÈNE HOPF

Dr. Mylène Hopf has dedicated her career to helping people live a long, active, and energetic lifestyle free of pain. After graduating Magna Cum Laude from Life Chiropractic College West in Northern California, Dr. Hopf joined the Vital Posture Clinic in 2010.

Being committed to providing the highest quality care and treatment means that Dr. Hopf continually furthers her education and knowledge, thus ensuring her clients receive the best service and care possible. Dr. Hopf has ongoing involvement with the National Upper Cervical Chiropractic Association (NUCCA), is completing a three-year Diplomate in Upper Cervical Procedures, and is actively engaged with both the Alberta and Saskatchewan Chiropractic Associations. She is also very involved with concussion management and awareness and is working towards providing appropriate training and education to other health care providers, sports associations, trainers, coaches, and teachers to help control the high prevalence of this potentially devastating injury.

www.drhopf.com

Home Is In Your Heart

By Colette Smithers

This beautiful, strong Irish woman is not the face I would envision when I think of homelessness. However, Colette not only conquered her situation, she tapped into her life lessons and became a strong, empathetic leader. The road to her castle had many bumps and curves, but she is now a Queen who rules with understanding and compassion.

BETWEEN 2006 AND 2009, I divorced, became estranged from my daughter, bought a house and lost it in foreclosure. My business was in my home, so that disappeared along with the house. I got rid of everything I owned, and at 49 years old, I moved in with my parents in Calgary.

I quickly jumped at the opportunity to work at the BC Winter Games. It was my chance to run away and escape from the past three years. I purposely cut myself off from everyone, including my siblings. They had not seen or heard from me in months.

When I returned to Calgary, I had planned to work with a girlfriend, revamping her business and renting one of her properties. That plan did not work out as I had envisioned. On May 10, 2010, I had the rug pulled out from under me when two of my sisters arrived to inform me that my girlfriend had contacted them to remove me from her house or she would have the police evict me!

I left with my sisters and went to one of their homes, and by early evening, all five of my siblings arrived. It appeared I was the subject of an intervention! Their 'talk' went something like this:

Colette, you're homeless, you're squatting, you have no job and no income. You have screwed up your life for the past few years and it's time to fix it. You must promise to sign up with a temporary agency tomorrow and get a job. You also have to have a complete mental assessment. They designated a sister-in-law to take me for that assessment.

The following morning I saw a psychologist at the Sundance Health Centre. I invited my sister-in-law to sit in because I had nothing to hide and I knew she would have to report back to *the posse.* After I talked for about 45 minutes, the psychologist excused herself, then returned to the room 15 minutes later. She moved her chair in front of me, put her hands on my knees, and said:

Colette, I have been working with our emergency housing team, looking for a bed for you. You cannot return to your sister's. It is not safe for you there. Another rug was pulled out from under me! My sister-in-law drove me back to my sister's house where I collected my things, and then she dropped me off at respite housing. That was the last time I saw or spoke with any of my siblings for the next two years.

After a brief stay in respite housing, I got a bed at the YWCA Mary Dover House where I lived for the next five months. The first three weeks were challenging. At that time, new residents had to spend 21 days in the dorm, a 12 x 20 room with three sets of bunk beds end-to-end down one wall and six locked dressers down the opposite wall. Curfew was 10:30 pm, at which time two YWCA staffers did a head count and turned the lights out. On my first night in the dorm, only the top bunks were available. I climbed the ladder to a bunk, fully dressed, laid down facing the wall and cried myself to sleep.

The next day, there was a 'post-it' on the dorm door directing me to meet with a caseworker for my 'intake'. The caseworker was 12 years old! This young girl, with pen in hand, bangs covering her face, and a stack of forms piled in front of her, was charged with getting *my life* back on track. How could she possibly relate to my circumstances? I left that meeting feeling utterly exposed, vulnerable, small and weak, like an inmate. My facial expression must have spoken volumes because when I returned to the dorm, two of the women, Carole and Maggie, told me not to worry. They promised to take me to social services to sign up for assistance. The next day, I signed up for welfare.

After three weeks in the dorm, I moved into a shared room. I spent the next few months trying to regain a sense of normalcy in my life. I stayed fit by walking around a nearby river while listening to my praise and worship music or pastor's messages on my iPod. I cooked and baked every day in the community kitchen and babysat for the young moms. I got to know the women — the glorious, caring, giving, brave, courageous, creative, funny, strong, tenacious, and beautiful women — my sisters at the YWCA.

I was surprised to discover that only one of about 80 women I encountered at the YWCA, was battling issues of alcohol and drugs. The majority of women were dealing with mental health, physical health, divorce, fleeing violence and abuse, immigration, lack of employment and lack of affordable housing issues. However, the one experience we had in common, our 'crime' so to speak, was poverty.

Here are just a few of the memories I have from the women I met at the YWCA:

Carole, 53, a university graduate and fierce feminist, was from New Brunswick. After her 20-year marriage failed, she left the small-town life and restaurant she had run with her husband, and moved to start over in Calgary. She worked in housekeeping in several hotels and shortly after leaving the YWCA, she became resident manager at one of the YWCA apartment buildings. Once a week, Carole and I enjoyed lively conversations over a glass of wine at the Marriott.

Maggie, a young native woman, was so quiet and tried desperately to be invisible. A photo of her daughter, who had been apprehended by Child Services, was taped on the bedpost to inspire her to keep fighting against drinking and taking drugs so that she could bring her baby girl home.

Jaylene, a tall, skinny, 'motor mouth,' chain smoker with a contagious laugh, made a movie star entrance into the dorm one night at 10:45 pm. YWCA had given her permission to break curfew so she could attend her daughter's grade 12 graduation. Jaylene had been released from hospital the day before, where she was recovering from an assault by her partner that left her with serious injuries, including the puncture of her left breast implant with a hammer. Three months later, Jaylene invited me to her graduation for completing a computer course she had taken at the Drop-In Centre. The Centre held a picnic at Prince's Island Park where diplomas were presented and a class picture was taken for the Drop-In Centre wall. I gave Jaylene a packet of cigarettes as a graduation gift.

On another evening, Jaylene told me Aziz was concerned because her grey hair was showing, and asked if we could colour her hair. Aziz was about 41 and from Pakistan. She had immigrated to Calgary with her husband and two teenage sons. She didn't speak English. The first time I met her, I said '*hello.*' She immediately took a photograph from under her sari, held it out to me and spoke in Pakistani. Crying, she hugged the picture to her heart and finally collapsed into my arms, sobbing. I learned that her husband had thrown her out and she couldn't see her sons. Immigration was trying to help her get support from her husband and access to her children.

At the drug store, Jaylene and I enjoyed a good laugh, pretending we didn't understand what Aziz wanted and we bought platinum blonde hair coloring. We sneaked some jet black colour into the bag and had great fun in the washroom colouring Aziz's hair. Aziz was a good sport and gifted me the most beautiful pair of sandals.

Ibeth, a 22-year-old Middle Eastern woman and devout Muslim, left her family in Calgary because her father refused to let her attend university. She attended the University of Calgary full-time, and spent the rest of her time studying or in prayer. She was afraid that her father might discover where she was and feared for her life.

Sharon was in her fifties and struggled with depression and anxiety. She was a genuine hippy flower child, who found peace and solace writing songs and playing her guitar. Sharon didn't like any of us '*bitches.*' She liked to be alone, but her beautiful voice — sometimes fiercely angry, sometimes heartbreakingly sad — echoed through the fourth floor halls as she poured out her soul in her songs.

I had been at the YWCA about four months when Gail and Val from the housing department asked to meet with me. Two things struck me about this meeting; first that Gail and Val were around my age, and second, it was just the three of us in the room. There were no computers, no forms, no desk, no phones; just a couple of coffee mugs on the table and three comfortable chairs. When I sat down, Gail said, "*So Colette, how are you?*" That simple question completely broke me. Suddenly, all the hurt, loss, betrayal, pain, and heartache of the past few years came pouring out in convulsive waves of grief. For so long, I had been a problem to be fixed, a case to be managed, an embarrassment to my family. I was alone and lonely. I told my story without blame or judgment, and left it all behind me in that room. I don't know how long we were in that room, but I do know that I was a different person when I came out. From that day on, I began to rise from the ashes of my life.

On the one Christmas I spent at the YWCA, a friend gave me a little embroidered picture and the words in the picture ring so true for me now. It says, *'Home is in your heart.'*

ABOUT COLETTE SMITHERS

Colette Smithers was born in Ireland and immigrated to Canada at age 16. She became a typical middle class Canadian woman: a wife and mother with a successful career.

At age 50, following a difficult divorce and the failure of her business venture, Colette found herself homeless, broke and alone. That experience, particularly her time spent with the women of the Calgary YWCA Mary Dover House, completely transformed her perception of faith, family, and home. She believes now in living life on her own terms, with empathy, gratitude, and joy.

Colette is passionate about the issue of homelessness for women and shares her story to encourage all of us to see each other as human beings, deserving of respect and dignity.

Colette is an avid foodie, amateur photographer, a novice trader, and budding writer. She is also the Director of Women Talk in Medicine Hat, Alberta.

www.facebook.com/colette.smithers
www.linkedin.com/in/colette-smithers-60638780

From Breakdown, Comes Breakthrough!

BY BRENDA FRAME

Adaptation is a skill Brenda has mastered. Not only can she adapt to new working situations in her life, but she is also able to fit into any group with great ease. When Brenda enters a room, the first thing I always notice is her larger than life, beaming smile! She is full of life and loves to take others on adventures that will energize them and make them feel full of life too.

Brigitte

MY HUSBAND AND I are currently manoeuvering a layoff. This isn't our first time. We've done this twice before and we've learned a thing or two along the way. Lessons learned have assisted us in moving from feeling fearful and victimized to feeling excited about possibilities for our future. I hope that some of our lessons learned can assist you.

Two of the three layoffs we experienced occurred while we were raising our family. Each of these lasted for a year and a half. The most recent one happened when we were in our late 50's, during a long economic downturn.

When the first layoff occurred, we quickly discovered that traditional job-hunting strategies of networking, relationships, and 'meeting the manager' were outdated and replaced with key words, search engines, and competing against hundreds if not thousands of other applicants. It felt really impersonal and frustrating to be prescreened by a computer.

Frustration with the process was soon coupled with frustration in our relationship. Our roles of caregiver and provider weren't as clearly defined, and that left me feeling angry and scared. I was frustrated that I had given up my professional income when I became an 'at home mom'.

I was angry at my husband for not finding a job. I was nervous about our escalating debt and I was scared at what all these feelings were doing to our relationship. I didn't want to add to the tension in our home, and felt like I couldn't talk about my concerns with anyone. It was a very challenging time.

What I learned from that experience was the importance of communication and of having a plan. My husband and I had both fallen into the trap of withdrawing and being fearful. I now know the better strategy of reaching out to others and allowing them to help me focus on what I am grateful for, to brainstorm options together, and to have them remind me of my value. I also realized that women process setbacks differently than men. Men need to quickly find solutions. Women need to talk and unload their emotions before searching for a solution and plans become obvious. It's very important to have a sounding board during a layoff.

When the second layoff occurred, we were offered a significant severance package. Unfortunately, one week before it was to be paid out, the company filed for bankruptcy protection. Severance packages weren't paid, pensioners discovered they were underfunded, and people on long-term disability got cut off completely! It felt like a kick in the teeth to the employees. It was a huge lesson in where a corporation's loyalty often lies. Our lesson learned was that severance packages and pensions aren't something to count on anymore in today's world.

With this second layoff, I was determined to not feel depressed and helpless again. Unnecessary expenses were quickly cut and we started creating income from several part-time jobs. Between running a network marketing business, hosting students in our home, and teaching first aid courses, I was a very busy girl for the next year and a half as Dave searched for his next job. When he found it, I didn't know whether to laugh or cry. I was so tired, so relieved, and so happy.

What I learned from that layoff is that working hard at multiple jobs is not a long-term solution. Having a job is a good solution for covering bills, but it's not an ideal solution for long-term freedom or security.

Through my involvement in the network marketing industry, I was introduced to the concepts of leverage and residual income. I decided that they were both critical components for the lifestyle and security that I desired. I also learned that the opportunity for freedom offered by different network marketing companies varies dramatically from one company to another. My first company had great products but despite being actively involved for twelve years, I never developed more than a modest part-time income with them. Rather than giving up on the industry, I chose to find a new company with a stronger compensation plan.

It took some searching, but I found it. The plan wasn't easy, but it paid well for someone willing to work hard. I knew I could do that! I figured nothing was harder than what we had done on the first two layoffs. Within three years, I had developed a growing team and a full-time income. Our secondary revenue stream was now in place.

The third layoff came with a new challenge. The economy was slow, with over 10% unemployment in our city. My husband was 57 and competing for jobs against thousands of younger applicants. We knew too well that another job search process would be a recipe for stress.

The older I've gotten, the more I have come to believe that life is about much more than working. The thought of working until we are 65 so that we can have a few years to enjoy life with an aging body and a small pension is beyond ridiculous in my mind. I wanted Dave to live a more fulfilling life rather than settle into yet another job.

We had recently become grandparents, we had aging parents in another province that we wanted to support, and we had a dream of running a retreat centre located in nature by a lake. We were tired of delaying our dream because of job commitments, and we made a bold decision to make choices that aligned with the life we truly want.

We decided to see Dave's final layoff as a gift rather than a loss, and to celebrate the opportunities that it opened for us. Having the income we had developed from my network marketing business helped make that decision possible.

We got creative and thought outside of the box as we put together a plan for our future. We came up with a combination of my network marketing business, a mentoring business that supports people in transition, and a bed and breakfast venture in our home. At first glance, they may seem like three separate projects, but there is one thing they have in common. They give us three unique ways to support people in living a life filled with what they care about the most. They allowed Dave and I to embrace our joint passion of supporting and empowering people.

Through network marketing, I can show parents how they can be home with their kids while also building another stream of income to reduce the financial stress. I can show people how to escape from the corporate world with an income that outstrips most pension plans. Network marketing is my vehicle to help people live a life of choice and freedom. It has been such a gift in our lives and we are happy to support others in learning how to benefit from it as well.

Through my mentoring business called "Transition with Clarity" I get to put my creative, problem-solving abilities to work as I help people gain clarity around an issue, come up with creative options, and then choose a solution that is the best match to what they value. Sometimes clients just need someone to bounce ideas off! I know I desperately needed that while dealing with the first two layoffs.

Finally, the bed and breakfast is unique in that our guests are people who are supporting someone in a nearby hospital. By reducing stress for our guests, they can be a stronger support for their loved ones in the hospital.

These three ventures complement each other and fit around how we want to live our life. They are also in alignment with making our long-standing dream of opening a retreat centre come true. Our centre will be a safe and comforting place for people to process their ideas and re-connect with what they want to do going forward, so that life once again feels fun and rewarding.

Life gives us opportunities to learn new lessons. I believe it is our obligation and privilege to "pay it forward" and use those lessons to help others successfully navigate through challenges and become stronger in the process.

I can't encourage you enough to take the time to consider what you really want to do or experience in your life. Get clear on what excites you and warms your heart. It will become the compass for decisions that you make and the people you attract. If you need help to reconnect with that, hire a mentor or a coach. You aren't here to live someone else's life or to make someone else wealthy. You are here to leave your own unique imprint on the world. You can only do that if you follow your passion and do something that truly matters to you.

ABOUT BRENDA FRAME

Brenda Frame loves to mentor and guide people as they incorporate what is truly important to themselves, back into their lives. She believes that life can feel exciting and fulfilling if you are willing to consider creative solutions and engage in the process of creating the life experience you desire.

She has worked as a physical therapist, trainer and coach. She has been a full-time 'stay at home' mom. After her family experienced several challenging layoffs, she became an entrepreneur. Brenda now combines three ventures that support her quest for a lifestyle of freedom, choice and the ability to empower others to take ownership of their lives.

Her mentoring business:
www. brendaframe.com

Her network marketing business:
www.breandaframe.nsopportunity.com

Her way of supporting others in need:
www.firesidebb.ca

One Step at a Time

By Heidi Cabay

Heidi's impact on my life is deep. Her gut-wrenching, murderous story has sent me on a quest to find out what makes people victorious. Ever since Heidi TALKed, I have wondered how is it even possible that this beautiful, positive, strong woman could have suffered such agonizing physical and mental pain. Her story will be with me forever.

HAVE YOU EVER allowed yourself to fully surrender to grief and forgiveness? Have you found the hope that is possible on the other side? The love available for the trees, the sun, and the moon. Love for music, movement, children, our mothers and fathers, all human connections. Most importantly, how would your life change if you forgave and loved yourself, mind body and soul?

I have spent 33 years of my life feeling lost, invisible, alone, and living with fear, but choosing to fight for freedom requires endless endurance and hope. And all for what? For love.

I was born grieving, but aren't we all? The loss of the safe warm womb. The home of a rhythmic echo from our mother's heart, the sweet soothing vibration of her voice and the safety of being swaddled inside her is torn away with our first entrance into the world and becomes our first exposure to loss. It took me a long time to realize that my primary emotion comes from the fact that I was born grieving. My traumatic childhood was smothered in grief and trauma stained my adolescence. My mother, Lisa, was murdered by my father when I was 17. The shame and stigma of who I was and what I was born into was the only life I knew. It felt like I lived in a dangerous and unpredictable tornado of deep-rooted suffering with tumultuous winds beating at me and stealing my breath.

My adult life became all about holding onto hope, but I was living in fear of never feeling protected or loved.

I am a runner, and have been my whole life. One crisp, sunny morning, I laced up my trusty "sole mates" and headed out on an old country road. Suddenly, a message bubbled up from my heart. It sparkled like a beam of sunshine and delivered a new thought pattern altering an old belief. *The opposite of fear is hope, not love.* I have never given up hope. Hope to find and feel love. I had chosen to live a life of love and I was choosing love, out of fear. Fear of grief, fear of pain, and fear of not being worth it.

As I ran, I thought about my three precious babies: my beautiful, kind and gentle daughter — my sunshine. My gentle, hardworking, always seeking, balanced boy — my sun. My sweet, nature-loving, make you laugh until your belly hurts little boy — my sunny. I felt how much love I have for them and how pure and unconditional it is. If they were absent or lost from my life, I would not be afraid, I would grieve, soul-wrenching grief. I couldn't help but ask myself, why as a girl, as a daughter, as a woman did I not feel love? I had love for life, love for special people and love for myself, but it was all formed to counteract my fear. The only love I had without fear was the love I felt for my children. I didn't feel whole. Choosing love and forcing it to counteract fear still didn't make me feel whole.

As a child, my home was draped in silence with alcohol, manipulation, violence, and control. I lived in fear and shame that this is what family life meant. I survived the horrors of emotional, sexual, and physical abuse culminating in murdering violence, only to later experience slipping through the cracks of a broken system that fails to protect victims' basic human rights. My father served ten years in prison, and six years of slow integration back into society, for a second-degree murder charge with a life sentence. I had been given ten years to create the life I wanted before I was vomited back into the filth of the system, a system that was my father's accomplice in the first place by not protecting my mother from being murdered. After seven crippling parole hearings, and the Parole Board of Canada acknowledging that this man is only a threat to women and his own children and not the general population, they chose to release him on full parole to retire comfortably into the community of his choice.

One might think that this would be enough to surrender to the tumultuous winds of the trauma tornado, to just be another statistic among abuse survivors who lead miserable lives. Enough to give up on the one thing that saved me for years — running — and never let my soul get laced up again, but it wasn't.

I was angry and completely empty from fighting for my own freedom and protection. I was in a complete state of surrender. There is significant truth in J.K. Rowling's words, "rock bottom became the solid foundation on which I rebuilt my life." Rock bottom was the beginning of me doing the opposite of what I had done in the past. I began taking up space to grieve, allowed myself to sit in my loss, sit in my pain and sit in my brokenness. I am a strong woman and my superpower of resilience and endurance that I wore like a superhero cape has carried me through a war which sought to define me. The moment I knew that the Parole Board decided that my safety and life was not worth protecting, my passion to keep my superwoman cape in flight was shattered and completely extinguished. It was in that darkness, that I untied the strings and turned my cape around to blanket myself. I blanketed myself with swaddles of love that a young baby, a young girl, and a woman deserves. Inside that gentleness of self-care, acceptance of my past and loss was graced with the warmth of my own blanket, my own love, healing.

It was like Newton's third law of motion, "for every action there is an equal and opposite reaction." My opposite reaction was to hit the road and let my footfalls ground me. Our energy, which cannot be created or destroyed, combined with our free will and purpose, allows us to choose our path through equal and opposite reactions. We are created for a higher purpose, but our choices determine our journey. This was like my first breath entering the world. The cry and scream of being born echoed down the long country road and ignited my lungs and pierced my heart with joy and love. I was alive.

I am in love with the power of opposites. It would've been easy to give up on my life and my own freedom. However, I chose the opposite. If alcohol, abuse, and control were all I knew, I chose the opposite. Love, kindness, gentleness, and healthy habits such as exercise and movement. I chose to be addicted to the endorphins of running instead of drugs. I made it my identity to be playful, live in the moment, and to make people smile and feel loved. This pattern of survival was all I had, the only way to prevent surrendering to the pain. I needed to choose love.

Over the many miles down country roads that my feet have carried me, one step at a time, little roots of connection and pathways from my head and heart began to attach. The deeper I reconnect my mind and soul within my body, the deeper the connections I have in my relationships with others. Bonding within myself started to allow pathways of healing to form, and they will stay forever empowering. They fill my veins with forgiveness, peace, grace, and deep love. Forgiveness for the horror, forgiveness to the holes in the systems, the authorities and the people who did their best at the time, and those who turned a blind eye because of self-preservation or policy. Forgiveness for the ones who can only empathize to the level of grief they've known in their own lives. Forgiveness for the great loss I have endured. Forgiveness for not knowing how to grieve. Peace, for doing the best I knew how and for never giving up hope. Grace, for the relationships that have blessed my journey for a short time or a lifetime.

Who we are, our journeys leaving footprints one step at a time, is our gift to the world. Survival is science, but being alive is the quest, I believe, all human beings seek. Allowing your soul to feel grief will set your heart free to feel love. Your head can choose it, your heart must bear it, and your soul needs to dance in it.

As Leanne Womack's heavenly voice sang, and was my mother's last wish for her girls, *I finally get it Mom*: "When you get the choice to sit it out or dance, I hope you dance." *Dance in love.*

ABOUT HEIDI CABAY

Heidi is an endurance expert. She chose from a young age to live not as a victim, but as a survivor. Persevering through innate strength and courage, she has rewritten the ending to the horror story which sought to define her, embracing the miracle of who she was created to be. Hers is a story of complexity, grief, strength, healing, forgiveness, resilience, fun, joy, and connection. She has presented to Junior and Senior High Schools, Women's Shelter Charity events, Law Enforcement, Educators, Victim Services, Homicide and Domestic Violence teams, Murdered and Missing Persons conferences, Aboriginal and Metis Murdered and Missing Women, Women Talk, Western Canada Victims of Homicide Conference, and various inspirational conferences. Her passionate spirit is infectious and it shows with her connections and love for people, especially children. Proof that H.O.P.E. *(hold on purpose evolves)* leads to the one thing we all desire, love. She continues her journey to inspire and empower others to live one step at a time through love.

www.journeyfreedom.com
www.facebook.com/heidifreedom
www.twitter.com/heidicabay

Get Busy at Living

BY BONNIE EARL

This woman is a pillar of strength and a master of feelings. Life handed her devastating lessons that could have crushed her. However, she not only carried these lessons with incredible strength and determination, she turned her challenges into a powerful feminine energy that now radiates from her beautiful heart and makes her a fierce cheerleader of women everywhere. Bonnie is living a full, powerful and meaningful life that she loves sharing with others.

Brigitte

$\mathcal{E}$VERYWHERE I GO, I hear women sharing stories about everyday challenges and not-so-every-day challenges. They remind me that I am not alone. They remind me that we, as women, have courage, strength, and power that we barely know.

I know what it is like to be faced with an unbearable challenge. I know what it is like to have the rug pulled out from under my feet and not know if I could ever get back on solid footing. And, I know there are gifts to be found on the other side of the pain.

My husband Richard and I had been separated for over two years and had begun talking about divorce. Then we began talking again. Much to our then eleven and nine- year-old daughters' delight, we had a reaffirmation of our vows. Our family was back together as a family unit for one year, and then...

On October 12, 1994, my husband Richard and I sat in a neurologist's office. We were there to receive test results. The neurologist announced to Richard, "You have Amyotrophic Lateral Sclerosis, more commonly known as ALS. No known cause. No known cure. Best-case scenario, two and a half years. Sorry." The neurologist got up and walked out.

We were left sitting there stunned and shocked, and then fell into each other's arms sobbing uncontrollably.

We brushed away our tears. Like two zombies, we went shopping for wallpaper for our younger daughter Jacquelyn's bedroom in the new house that we were moving into in two weeks.

We went through the motions of the rest of our day. Once we tucked our daughters in bed, I stumbled to our bedroom, closed the door, dropped to my knees and prayed. With tears streaming down my face I asked, "Why? Why would you give me this beautiful family, only to tear us apart?" Over my sobbing, I heard a voice saying, "It's not yours to question why. It's yours to trust." A strange sense of peace washed over me, the kind that surpasses all understanding. I knew that somehow everything was going to be all right. I crawled into bed and fell asleep.

Unlike me, that night Richard stayed up all night. The next morning, he said to me, "I've been thinking. I have a choice when something like this happens. I can dig a hole and crawl into it. Or, I can live until I'm not alive. I'm going to get busy at living, not busy at dying."

On that morning, my trust and his choice to live merged. On the outside, our family didn't look much different.

We moved into our new house and made it a home. We told our daughters about Richard's ALS on a "need to know basis." I continued to work full-time and our daughters carried on with school and all their usual routines. Richard started medical leave.

As a family, we stayed busy with living. Richard loved to downhill ski so every weekend we hit the slopes with our daughters. Some days it was clear skies. Other days, it was a blizzard. It didn't matter. We golfed. We camped. We traveled. We went to our daughters' soccer, volleyball, and basketball games. We laughed. We cried. We took delight in family and friends. We savored the little things.

ALS continued to stalk us. Like a heartless thief, it robbed Richard of his ability to swallow. When eating became a marathon of futility, a feeding tube was installed directly into his stomach. I would crush up pills to control his salivating, adding them to his liquid food. After each feeding his stomach hurt.

When the pooling of saliva could no longer be controlled through pills, a home care nurse showed me how to do suctioning of the saliva out of his throat. This role terrified me. Yet, we were still a team. Richard would hold my hand and guide the tube down his throat. Together, every four hours, we did what needed to be done to prevent him from choking to death on his own saliva.

One morning, I was holding a towel for him as he stepped out of the shower. His beautiful tear-filled eyes caught mine and through slurred speech, he asked, "How can you love this drooling bag of bones?" My heart stopped. I looked into his eyes and I heard myself say, "I love you, your soul. You are not your body. I love YOU."

ALS stole Richard's ability to speak, but it didn't take away his ability to communicate. Richard learned to use sign language. The one he used most often was, "I love you." He wrote in his journal.

As a highly intelligent man who loved to talk, this was downright challenging. In a fit of anger Richard wrote, "You don't understand what it's like to not speak." I decided, "I want to know." I gave myself a challenge. I wrote at the top of my journal "Richard has ALS and cannot speak. I want to experience what this is like, and so I am not speaking." As I went about my errands that morning, the responses to my challenge were varied. Some people talked louder. Some people talked slower. Some took my journal and replied by writing in the journal. I came home after three hours, exhausted and with a whole new appreciation for Richard's experience AND the power of the written word.

When his muscles weakened, his scratchy handwriting became harder to read and his words became more precious.

By June of 1996, Richard's speech was unintelligible and his muscles feeble. We both knew that the time we had left together was short. His mom gifted us with an Alaskan cruise, a bucket list item for both of us. A song played in the dining room one night, where he came to enjoy the smells of the food he couldn't eat. His eyes filled with tears. "What's the name of that song?" I asked. He handed me this note:

"Fish got to swim
Birds got to fly
I got to love

One gal 'til I die
Can't help loving
That gal of mine"
—Irving Berlin

We hugged. We cried. We walked outside under the moonlight. He held me close as we swayed to the music. And time stopped. No words needed to be spoken. I felt his heart beat, his hand on my back. I saw his look of adoration. I knew I was cherished.

On that cruise, Richard wrote, "I need you home with me now." I took a leave of absence from my full-time work to honour his request.

Richard loved words. We spent hours playing Scrabble. He usually won. We both loved music and music was always playing in our home, from Dr. Hook, The Eagles, and Jackson Browne to Beethoven and Bach.

Richard chose to live and die at home.

On February 7, 1997, Pachelbel's Canon played in the background. I sat on our bed beside Richard. Our daughters, Jennifer and Jacquelyn, camped out at Richard's feet. The three of us sang, talked, and told stories. Richard gasped for every breath. Nothing was wrong. And everything was wrong. One final agonizing breath and then Richard was gone.

Richard's final entry in his journal read, "To my wife and children, know that you are loved."

And in that, we heard the truth. We knew that we were going to be all right. We had been brought closer together for sharing this ALS journey.

ALS was like a gift that came in ugly wrapping paper. It's what prompted me to take an early retirement from a fulfilling career in education, to work with women searching for themselves. My experience allows me to hold the space for women to simply be in their pain, whatever that pain is. I want you, the woman who holds this book in her hands, to know that whatever challenges you are facing:

You are magnificent.

You are bigger than any obstacle.

You get to decide how you respond to life's challenges and write the story of your life.

I want women to know that when we share what matters and why it matters, we create a huge opportunity for healing for ourselves, other women, and humanity. Sharing our thoughts and feelings is about creating a world of connection, caring, and healing for the whole planet.

After Richard died, my elder daughter, Jennifer said to me, "It's good that Dad loved you the way he did. You will have enough love to last you a life time." I draw on that love in the work I do now. I teach women that regardless of the circumstances they find themselves in they can create an empowering story that always lands on what's beautiful.

ABOUT BONNIE EARL

Bonnie Earl is a Women's Empowerment Coach and Speaker with a 35-year history in education. After her husband's death from ALS, she felt compelled to help women in pain, fear, and confusion to create a new, empowering chapter of their lives. She is masterful at holding space for women so that they know that regardless of their pain, they have a power that they can get to know.

Bonnie teaches a unique set of practices for a 'new' generation of women leaders who want to lead with their feminine side. She teaches women how to get out of their heads and into their bodies, to connect to their powerful and feminine energy so they can have a positive life and impact on others, as well as the ability to earn the income they desire.

Bonnie is a proud mother of two amazing daughters, and Nana of two incredible grandchildren.

www.bonnie-earl.com
www.facebook.com/bonnie.earl.9
www.twitter.com/BonnieEarl3

What's in A Name?

BY REHANA MALIK-MBANGA

Strength lies in our differences, not our similarities. Rehana is a beautiful representation of what women of multiple cultural backgrounds bring to our world. Surrounded by so many strong women from around the globe, Rehana has acquired knowledge that can't be taught in a classroom. As she enters a new phase of maturity in her life, she brings with her rich diverse teachings for others to learn from as well.

WOMEN AROUND THE globe have certain expectations placed on them from how to act and speak to what roles to assume in society. In North America's patriarchy, up until very recently (and some would argue even today), we've been expected to be obedient to our husband, assume caregiving roles even if we work outside the home, to make ourselves small to take up less space, and to speak softly, if at all. But what does a woman do if she comes from various cultural backgrounds all with a different set of rules? What if at her core a woman feels that she is meant to take up space, and be seen and heard?

Personally, I am a cultural mosaic with so many pieces of multi-coloured glass that I can't help but be a piece of art, but only if I let my light shine from within.

My father is the son of an Indian Muslim father and a bi-racial mother. My paternal grandmother's two races come from being the daughter of a Tumbuka mother from an Eastern Zambian Tribe and an Indian Muslim father who came from Pakistan with his brothers to start trading in Zambia. Confused yet? We're just getting started.

My mother's maternal grandmother was a bi-racial woman with an Italian father and Lenje mother from a Central Zambian tribe, whose father was a bi-racial man with a British father and an Ngoni woman from an Eastern Zambian Tribe. My maternal grandfather was a bi-racial man with a Jewish father from Lithuania and an Ndebele mother from a Zimbabwean Tribe.

My cultural background is Muslim, Christian, and Jewish, originating from Pakistan, Zambia, Italy, Lithuania, Great Britain, and Zimbabwe. And if that wasn't enough to confuse someone's identity, I have also lived in very different societies in Zambia, South Africa, Zimbabwe, Australia, and now Canada.

Therefore, I'm sure it doesn't come as a shock that I had to take a few moments to regroup myself and choose what role I would play in my marriage to a strong Shona African Christian man. It is common in Christianity and most parts of the world to take your husband's last name. I haven't always had a double barrel surname but I have been caught between two worlds, that of Islam and that of being a dutiful Shona wife.

In Islam, it is considered Haraam — the Islamic word for sin — to take a name other than your father's because a child belongs to her father and cannot belong to any other human being. And, to take your husband's name would mean you belong to him.

When I learnt this about Islam, I was so empowered to learn that contrary to many cultural practices, in some Muslim marriages, a woman was her own person and not property of her husband. Being the strong-headed independent woman I am, I adopted this part of my Muslim heritage and honoured my father by keeping the surname Malik.

When I decided that my now husband was *the one*, I decided to learn everything that I could about my heritage and take all the good parts and make them my culture. As I prepared for marriage, I decided to have a traditional Zambian wedding called Lobola to embrace my African heritage, a Mendhi night which is an East Indian rite of passage similar to a hen night, and finally a wedding in the Catholic church because my parents were married in the Catholic church and my husband and I were both confirmed Catholics.

The decision to embrace my heritage led to an unexpected event, and I will forever be grateful for the wisdom that was shared with me during this ceremony.

As I sat down on the floor in my late great-grandmother's house on our family farm in rural eastern Zambia where my father grew up, I was surrounded by a group of elderly women that were apparently relatives from my grandmother's village. They had come to socialize me into marriage the traditional way.

In the corner of the room was a single bed without a mattress or bedding on it. This was previously my great grandmother's room and had not been used by anyone since she had passed two years prior. A total of 14 women sat on reed mats called Mpasa on the varnished concrete floor. A single window opposite the door let sunlight into the dim room. As I sat down on the floor in my chitenge, a batik cloth around my waist, I could smell the floor polish that had been used to clean the room in preparation for the auspicious rite of passage. My aunt leaned over to me and asked me not to look anyone directly in the eyes, and to slightly put my head down as a sign of humility and respect of the elders in the room. We all said a quick prayer to thank God for my marriage.

The women spoke Nyanja, a language I could hardly understand even though my father and his siblings spoke it fluently. My Aunt Amina whispered the narrative in English for me and two of my already married friends that had been permitted to come with me. Only married women were allowed in this room because these teachings were a rite of passage into marriage. My heart pumped with joy because I felt so special, so humbled and amazed by the wisdom coming from these women's mouths.

I watched two ladies demonstrate how I should treat my husband and new family through song and dance while two ladies beat the drum. I listened attentively as each word empowered me with the tools on how to run my household, meal prep, look after my children, handle my in-laws, and how to balance my career and family life. "Remember your home must have peace," they said, "do not argue with your husband in front of anyone. Instead, cool down if you are angry and speak with him in your bedroom after he has also calmed down so your ears can both hear, not your emotions. When your in-laws visit, always show your best just as you would for your blood."

"Remember that a woman is everything, she is the queen. Nurture your husband and affirm him. Teach one another that his success is yours and your success is his. Do not belittle one another it will destroy your home." The advice went on for hours but I lingered on every word because I knew that it was important to learn. As I looked up to my aunts, I could see the pride in their body language as they ululated and danced with satisfaction that they had passed on the legacy of success.

This is a very exclusive initiation process in the Zambian culture and a married woman is always judged by how well she was taught during this process. It was on the floor in that room that I fully embraced my African heritage and own the African woman many have come to know today. That wisdom has been the secret recipe for the success of my married life and has allowed me to identify myself as a Zambian woman.

I remember how empowered I felt the night we celebrated my traditional marriage and I became Amai Mbanga which means mother of Mbanga children in Shona, my husband's language.

Many women struggle in marriage because we try to compete with our spouses. We think that mimicking male-like behaviour gives us power. We disrespect our spouses not realizing that we disrespect ourselves in the process because we misunderstand what it means to be a feminist. We forget how beautiful and empowering it is to be a woman. We stop dressing up, we stop grooming ourselves, we stop laughing, and the worst — we forget to love ourselves. I learned that men and women are different beings, we see the world differently, and we express this experience differently. I have observed it in my daughter and son before they even knew their gender. I encourage other women to work on who they are and together with our spouses to become better versions of ourselves.

I learnt that I am a woman and that means I am strong, unique, special, and beautiful. I have purpose.

I have since added Mbanga to my surname to honour my husband because he has honoured me by investing and supporting in my visions, but most of all because he is a man that falls in love with me over and over again. He has truly embraced everything I am, and I have embraced his culture. I also have to admit that the catalyst to using a hyphenated last name was being put on the back of an aircraft seat whilst my husband and children were seated up front because we had different surnames.

So, what is in a name? Definitely more than meets the eye.

Your cultural background may be as mixed as mine or quite pure. Either way, I hope you are inspired to have a look at the best practices from where you come from and make an empowered choice about who you choose to be in the world. May you be colourful, take up your full space, and speak your truth loudly for all to hear.

ABOUT REHANA MALIK-MBANGA

Rehana Malik-Mbanga is an entrepreneur with a psychology background who spends her days working with the chronically homeless in Edmonton. As diverse as Rehana's cultural background is, so are her career pursuits. She is currently helping Angelina Paul build a community called Open Communion sharing the untold stories of African Women with the world. An upcoming vlog with her sister Shamim Malik, called Coffee Time with Pana and Mima, shares their story of two African sisters living in diaspora. Rehana also has a blog that shares her journey as a plussize woman called Embracing Plus Sized Me. She is married to the love of her life and is the proud mom of two beautiful children. Rehana runs a consulting company with her husband that provides accounting and business coaching services. You can find out more about them at www.stimbok.com.

www.ocommunuion.com
www.facebook.com/panaandmima
www.facebook.com/embracingtheplussizeme

The Universe Has Plans For You!

By Sue Deyell

Her charm is magical, it shines through the radio, the television, in front of a crowd, or one on one. Sue has the gift of entertainment and nothing will keep her down. This witty word wizard has amused hundreds of thousands with her strong voice and presence, but she's not done yet. Next, she will take you away on an adventure with her plume.

WHO EVER THOUGHT getting fired would be a good thing? Not me. But it turned out it was, four times over!

I was a shy kid, but I always dreamed of being an entertainer. The day I discovered I could actually be a radio announcer, just like the DJ's I grew up listening to, my life changed, and I found my calling.

I started at my first on-air job in a small town with a population of 16,000, which ironically was also my first salary! I met life-long friends, learned my craft and I wouldn't change a thing.

In a short span of time, I went from an afternoon news announcer to Morning Show Co-Host and that's when I knew I was truly 'home', when it came to being on-air. I thoroughly enjoyed bantering with one or more people on a morning show. It was the perfect job for me, and ultimately, that's what I did for the next 20 years.

I was on my fourth radio gig when it happened. I was moving up in the world, moving to bigger radio stations and larger markets. So, when I was hired on the morning show of the #1 station in the city, I figured I had it made. It was a five-person morning show, and we were having a blast — both on and off the air.

One morning while I read my newscast on-air, the boys were kicking a big exercise ball like a soccer ball, and it hit me in the back of the head so hard my face bounced off the mic, my glasses went flying and all five of us erupted into hysterics. I never did finish that newscast.

So many things happen when the microphones are off, things the listener (fortunately or unfortunately) never gets to see or hear. But hopefully the fun the announcers are having together translates into fun for the listener too.

I worked for four years at one of the top radio stations in the market, and things were humming along until... I got fired.

I was devastated. I was embarrassed. I was hurt and angry. I kept asking myself why. I was where I was meant to be — doing what I was meant to do. I was happy to stay put, to keep on keepin' on. So when I got fired I took it personally — even though it had nothing to do with "me". It was a business decision and I was moved over to be part of a brand new radio station that was about to launch. An opportunity most radio announcers never get to be part of, a gift really.

In the end, it was a blessing in disguise... it really was a promotion, though I couldn't see it at the time.

I was happy with the status quo, never even thinking about "the next step". So, the next step was taken for me! Often in life we get complacent, even though, inside, we know there's more. Or maybe we don't see that until later. Hindsight is always 20/20.

I was having a blast working with a guy who became a great friend. I learned to run the control board myself, and "go solo" on the morning show. I was learning many new things outside my comfort zone — things I swore I had no desire to learn or do mainly because I had been afraid to try.

And then I got fired.

I wasn't expecting that one. Didn't see it coming. It hurt. The Universe clearly had bigger plans for me. Staying put is easy. Moving onwards is not.

A kick in the pants is usually a good thing. Yeah, your butt might hurt for a while, but when you open your eyes and look at it for what it is, you realize deep down you needed that nudge to move forward.

So be it. I nursed my bruised ego and guess what? The next job came looking for me! That's right Universe, bring it on. I joined another morning show at a rock station with two guys who became like brothers to me. Over the next three years, we had tremendous fun off and on-air, and took our listeners along for a brilliant ride.

I still get comments on that morning show to this day. Listeners still tell me how much they enjoyed our humour and camaraderie, and how they couldn't wait to hear what we'd say next.

I think that's one of the most special parts of being on the air.

You become part of people's lives, part of their everyday routine and they make room for you, and for what you have to share with them.

I learned some incredible things over my years on-air, about the people on the other side of the radio.

Listeners give you their valuable time. They tune in to hear what you have to say, so you'd better make it worthwhile, make it memorable, even if only for a brief couple of minutes.

I learned to do my homework, be intelligent, give them a laugh, make it fun for them, make them want to come back and listen to you again tomorrow morning.

Three years later, on a Monday morning, we read in the newspaper that some 'big name' dude from another city was taking over the morning show on our station. But wait... WE were the morning show! We went to our boss who swore it was a mistake and not to worry. Until the next day when they told us we were fired.

Radio is a crazy business. Firings and hirings happen all the time, but I wouldn't change my wacky 25-year career for anything. I have accomplished so much more than I dreamed possible. And I learned about my own strength and resiliency. I finally learned each time I got knocked down, the Universe was just propelling me to something bigger and better.

My next job was to launch yet another new radio station, but after a fabulously fun four-year run there... can you guess what happened?

Yup. Fired again. The entire on-air staff let go!

This time being fired led me out of my comfort zone, to an unspoken dream.

I got to host my own TV show!

I was the star, and the gist was that I got hired to work with companies who would teach me to do what they did. I was their surrogate employee. Now, let's just say I'm not terribly gifted at fixing or building things, so when I messed up, which I did a lot, it was pretty funny stuff!

I got the opportunity to try many jobs from plumbing to laying flooring, tearing up and repaving a driveway, landscaping, building cabinets (nail gunned my finger on that one) and I attempted to shingle a roof. I was a roofer who was afraid of heights, so to cure my fear, the owner of the company took me skydiving. Yes, skydiving! Check that off my bucket list.

I also learned how to pick and then cut marble and granite for countertops. To do that, the company took me to Italy to a mind blowing white marble quarry at the top of the French Alps. I couldn't really complain about getting fired from my last radio job when this was the consolation prize.

Yes, all good things must end, though for me, every "end" has been a fabulous new beginning.

It took me a while to see it, but everything in life happens for a reason. Every time there was bad, it was followed by good, and in fact by better. I've been knocked down and I've gotten back up.

Sometimes it's hard to see at the time, but you've just got to believe in yourself and not be afraid to take the next step.

So this time, I'm taking the next step on my own.

My true dream has always been to write books. I've dreamed of being a famous writer all my life, of being an author. I can even envision myself in my office, a small but cozy building tucked behind my beach house. Me sitting at my antique desk, in front of a big glass wall, overlooking the ocean, as waves crash onto the shore.

For a long time I believed being a writer was just a dream to be kept quiet, hidden deep inside, a dream I didn't dare say aloud for fear someone would laugh at me. But I'm not afraid to share my dream any more.

I don't need you to push me this time Universe, I got the point... all four times!

I don't want to look back one day, and say "what if"? I don't want to wonder what might have been, had I just taken a chance. I don't want it to ever be too late.

My message to you is this — life is short. Don't be afraid to fail. If you truly want something, you'll find a way to make it happen.

And remember, the Universe will always be there to give you a gentle nudge and a helping hand to propel you along the way!

Stay tuned for my next chapter....

ABOUT SUE DEYELL

The youngest of four children, Sue Deyell developed her gift of making others laugh early on as her way to get attention. It was only natural that a career in entertainment would follow the little girl whose favorite book growing up was a joke book.

Sue launched her career as a radio announcer more than 20 years ago, and has made a profession of sharing her sense of humour by putting an amusing spin on everyday life. Whether on-air or in front of a crowd, helping people see the funny side of life is always her goal.

Now Sue is switching things up and moving from the spoken to the written word. Stay tuned for the newest developments as Sue sits down to her keyboard with her incurable desire to entertain her readers and put a smile on their faces.

www.professionalmc.ca
www.suedeyell.com
www.facebook.com/sue.deyell.3
www.twitter.com/suedeyell

Who Am I?
Discovering Myself through Enneagram Personalities

BY EILEEN HEAD

Eileen might be small but she is mighty. She is focused and determined to make as many relationships thrive as she possibly can. I love how she can turn on the information tap, full flow, anytime, anywhere. I will forever be grateful to Eileen for introducing me to the Enneagram Personalities. Her marriage may not have succeeded but it's obvious to me that she will be saving many relationships, including mine.

*H*AVE YOU EVER felt disconnected from your family of origin?

In my family, I am the youngest, with three older brothers. I spent a lot of time wondering how to connect to my brothers and my parents. It felt like we were all individual planets rotating around each other and lost in our own little world. It wasn't until I learned about Enneagram (*pronounced any-a-gram*) Personalities that I was able to really understand our different personality perspectives.

I watched my parents as they stumbled their way through life, raising kids, surviving on a farm, and feeling confused with each other. When I met my future husband at 16, I was thrilled! Finally somebody just for me!

We were high school sweethearts and married at 18. I thought I had met my Prince Charming. We were married for 35 years and then divorced. What happened? We did everything right. We worked hard and were good parents.

Throughout our relationship, we had difficulty communicating with each other. My husband was my "silent" partner. He was quiet and didn't talk much, but I didn't know why. We focused on our kids and had a good life. On the outside looking in, many people believed we had a good marriage.

But I found myself yearning for something more and I asked myself, "Is this all there is?" I was unhappy. I believed it was his job to make me happy. That's what a partner is supposed to do, right?

I felt frustrated, alone and my husband was a complete mystery to me and I am sure I was a mystery to him too. I felt disconnected from him. He never shared what he was thinking or feeling nor did he include me in his hopes and dreams. We seemed more like business partners, each doing what we were best at and sharing a little affection now and then.

I couldn't figure out what I was doing wrong. I would spend many nights going over the day attempting to understand why he was distant or withdrawn. I would ask him what was wrong and he would say, "nothing." I felt helpless. Both our families had a similar pattern of behaviour — we would disconnect, sometimes for days in strained silence.

I felt the distance and would question myself. Was I saying too much, not saying enough, should I be saying it differently? Just tell me what is going on! The silence was almost unbearable.

My insecurities would be triggered with feelings that I "was not good enough." I was so stressed that at times I would burst into tears in the grocery store or while driving home.

I needed him to talk, to share and to appreciate me for what I felt were the loving things I did for him. Whenever I would attempt to share with him how I was feeling, he would shut down and withdraw.

My husband spent a lot of time with his hobbies and working and seemed content. He didn't appear to need the emotional connection like I did. I spent a lot of time attempting to unravel the mystery of our relationship. I could not make sense of why we could not relate to one another. If I knew what he needed I would happily give it to him but he didn't appear to know either.

I saw other couples who seemed to have their own language. They looked comfortable and happy with each other and you could feel the great energy between them.

I would wonder, "What's The Secret? Why Can't I Figure Us Out?"

I desperately searched for answers to the Why by reading stacks of self-help books and marriage manuals and taking courses.

Time passes quickly and before I knew it, it was our 25th Anniversary. I would see other couples renew their vows or go away on a special vacation. My husband agreed to a weekend away and I was very excited to spend time together.

Our anniversary was a huge milestone for me and I had expectations on how the weekend would go, with declarations of love and connection. I had asked him if he would buy me a small gift as a keepsake. When we got to the hotel, he told me he had been working too hard and hadn't had time to buy a gift. Although disappointed, I didn't want anything to spoil the weekend with a fight or moodiness and replied, "That's okay, you can get me something downtown."

We went downtown and I thought I would make this really easy for him. We stopped at the Christmas Store and I said, "Would you go in there and buy me a Christmas decoration?" I thought that would be a great keepsake for years to come.

His answer was, "NO!" What did he say? Did he just say "no?" All the years of frustration and disappointment welled up inside me and I planted my back foot, grabbed the lapels of his coat and commanded, "You are going to go in there and buy me something!" and I pushed him through the door.

I stood there feeling immense shame that I had to use physical force to get him to buy me some little thing. It turns out he was very excited with the decorations he had selected but I just wanted to throw them on the ground and stomp on them. Did I speak up when he came out of the store? No, I swallowed it down. If I had spoken up, I might have learned that he wanted to buy me something else and it would have changed the destiny of both of our lives. That was our pattern, not dealing with issues.

We settled for a flat relationship for another ten years until I came to the point of, "I need to leave you for me." When we can find no answers, we give up. I felt out of integrity living with a man I no longer loved.

As I left the marriage I found the Enneagram Personalities. Discovering our profiles was the biggest A-Ha moment of my life. In 30 minutes, I knew more about my husband, myself and our relationship than in the

35 years we had lived together. I found the answers I was searching for. We didn't understand our personalities or our "couple dynamics."

Here is a little bit of what I learned about our two personalities after I discovered the Enneagram. I am a 2 — Supporter and my previous husband is a 9 — Peace Seeker.

A Supporter's basic need is for connection and sees themselves as loving fixers who can make other's lives easier. They put aside their own needs to focus on their partner. Supporters overdo their giving and, in order to feel valued, intrusively help.

A Peace Seeker's basic need is to stay peaceful, feel the intensity and react to maintain their independence by procrastinating, becoming distracted, and resisting going along with the plan through passive-aggressive behaviour. They feel expectations are too high and did not want what is being given in the first place.

Supporters need intimacy and need to share their thoughts and feelings. Peace Seekers fear that stating their own needs will cause conflict and remain silent to keep peace. This means Peace Seekers become frustrated as their own needs are never met either.

Supporters intensify their efforts and pressure Peace Seekers to express their feelings, attempting to wring out emotions. Peace Seekers see this as a demand and respond by withdrawing and giving the silent treatment. This is felt as severe punishment to the Supporter.

I had been laser focused on this relationship to fix us and later learned this is what was driving us apart. For his personality, the intensity was too high and his harmony was disturbed.

This is the dance we carried on for 35 years, only we couldn't see the patterns. I would reach out and he would retreat. I would feel rejected and hurt and he would feel inadequate and in conflict.

Now that I understand it was our personality patterns, I can now see how we misread and misunderstood each other. Neither of us knew how to get our needs met to feel loved or how to love each other.

If we had known how our personalities were affecting our relationship, and how we could respond more lovingly, it might have saved our marriage.

I didn't know myself or what I needed to feel loved and appreciated.

Until you truly know that, you will never be happy in any relationship. Most importantly, I learned to love and accept myself — even the challenging parts. I now know what gifts I bring to my relationships, how I contribute to the world, and how to get loved the way I need to feel loved.

In searching for relationship answers, I found my passion and purpose which is fully aligned with my personality's basic instinct. As a Personality and Relationship expert, it brings me great joy to help others unravel the mysteries and dynamics of all their relationships.

ABOUT EILEEN HEAD

 Eileen Head is a Personality & Relationship Expert, International Bestselling Author of "Why Can't I Figure Us Out?" Coach, Speaker, and Workshop Facilitator. Through her coaching and workshops, she assists people with "figuring themselves out" and how to become their best self. She then empowers them by teaching them about such powerful tools as the Enneagram (any-a-gram) Personalities to find their Relationship Answers.

Eileen is committed to getting you the life and love you need to find happiness. She assists people to create connected and loving relationships with a couples' online program called Get Loved The Way You Need, choosing your perfect mate through Singles Guide to Personality Matching, and how to understand and get along well with others. Eileen coaches people personally and professionally to understand themselves better and make sense of all their relationships.

www.eileenhead.com
www.facebook.com/EileenHeadConsultant

From People-Pleaser to Me-Pleaser

By Darlis-Keily Ireland

This small, red-haired Irish woman is full of life. As one of my Women Talk Directors and emcee, I get to enjoy Darlis' fabulous presence monthly on the mic. She may have spent a good part of her life pleasing others but now it's with a big smile on her face and a twinkle in her eye that she empowers and challenges us to be all we can be.

Brigitte

"The light of my own being guides my life forward."
— Anonymous

$\sim$

*H*AVE YOU EVER looked at your life and wished parts, or all of it, had been different?

Have you deliberately behaved a certain way to avoid rejection?

Have you wondered who you truly are?

This was my life for 44 years, then *I found the light.*

Let's start at my beginning...

An only child, I was raised in small-town Saskatchewan by entrepreneurial parents. Our home was located in the back of their business, which meant Main Street was my playground and the shopkeepers were my playmates.

I was teased relentlessly by my cousins, spent a lot of time alone, and had violent temper tantrums. My child-brain decided that my feelings, needs, and my very existence were of little value. I felt overlooked, misunderstood, and certainly not special or even lovable. To protect myself, I turned off my emotions and logic became my new ally.

In my efforts to be accepted, I became very good at assessing situations and behaving how I believed others wanted me to be. I developed strong communication skills to ensure I said what people wanted to hear. Entering my teenage years, everything I did was influenced by my fear of being rejected. To please the adults, I was a high achiever in school and well-known in the community. On weekends, the party girl came out in full force, and yet, I never felt like I belonged in either world.

I had no clue who I was or what I wanted. Good heavens, I went to university to please my family and chose pre-law because a teen magazine article said the shape of my ears meant I would be a great lawyer!

In my first year of school, the rebelling (self-destruction) began with alcohol and drugs. By year two, I was rarely going to school and realized I was in yet another place I didn't belong. I dropped out.

So what do you do if you are not in school? *Why, you get married!* I was convinced that if I wasn't married by my 23rd birthday, I would die old and alone. This thought terrified me and as a result, I said "I do" (four months before I turned 23) to a man I knew I wasn't in love with.

After recovering from my third bout of post-partum depression, I received what I now refer to as a 'divine download' and I absolutely knew I had to go back to school. I enrolled, I gave birth to our fourth child and I graduated at the top of my class. To avoid my marriage, I became a workaholic while my husband was a very committed stay-at-home-dad to our children. After 14 years, I finally found the courage to admit that I didn't belong in the marriage and we amicably parted ways.

I was still seeking acceptance and to gain it, I worked 80 hours a week, tirelessly volunteered and maintained a social life while being a single parent during some extremely difficult times. I became physically, mentally, and spiritually exhausted.

Depression settled in, but since I had been doing personal development work for 15 years, I knew I could self-recover. Well, it was such a good story that I actually believed it! Unfortunately, that recording from childhood kept playing deep in my subconscious: *"Suck it up. Work harder. Do what others need you to do and people will accept you... then you'll be happy."* So, like the seven dwarfs in the fairy tale, I put on a smile and sang, "Hi Ho Hi Ho, it's off to work I go."

Two years passed. I endured two more assaults of depression and then I hit rock bottom. I knew something had to change but I didn't know who I was or what I wanted. I didn't know what to do except cry. And so day after day after day, that's what I did.

Then someone I trust, who had seen enough of my suffering, said, "Get serious and do *real* inner work. Do something that will make a difference!" Since I wasn't capable of making decisions for myself, I agreed to go to a Body Energetics retreat in British Columbia.

Body Energetics, I quickly discovered, involves very loud, expressive and intense behaviour as a way of getting in touch with your emotions. *Are you serious?* I spent my entire life ignoring my emotions. Emotions hurt. Emotions got me in trouble. Emotions were bad. Logic kept me safe, and now here I was in a room of apparent looney tunes that wailed, swore, yelled, moaned, and hit things with ferocious anger. I had signed up for Camp Crazy! I was horrified, terrified, and completely ashamed of *their* behaviour. There was no doubt that I was the only normal person there.

The first three days, I desperately wanted to be invisible and I refused to participate. I wanted off that island, but at the same time, I couldn't bring myself to leave. The facilitator was respectful of my 'invisibility cloak' and I slowly began to participate in our daily sharing circles. On day four, in the midst of my tentative sharing, I was shocked when she asked how it felt growing up with an alcoholic father. *My dad wasn't an alcoholic!* She restated parts of my story, and as I fearfully looked at the faces around me, it was clear they agreed with her. *An alcoholic? Had my father really been an alcoholic?* Confusion and sadness washed over me. Could it be that I was so focused on being my dad's favorite person in the world, that I was blind to his truth? How could I not know? What was wrong with me?

She invited me into her arms. *Are you friggin' kidding me? A stranger holding me in a room of strangers that scare the hell of me? That would be so embarrassing!* My body betrayed my mind and I scooted over and curled up in her arms like a small child. She began to rock me and spoke barely above a whisper. She told me I was loved. I was special. I was wanted. And a river of tears began to flow down my sad face.

I sobbed as wave after wave of grief poured out. They pulled over a mattress and for hours, I lay curled up while these looney tune strangers took turns being with me. They held me, telling me how I was loved, wanted, cared for and so very special. That afternoon, I turned my emotions back on and officially became a looney tune whose life had finally begun.

For the remaining three days, I cried. I cried when people looked at me. I cried when I saw the buffet. I drank water and yes, I cried. And when I got home, I lay in bed for three days shedding more tears as I let go of the old me. On day four, I got out of bed with a clear head, determined to change my life.

Someone wise once told me the best decisions are those that bring you closer to pleasure rather than those that avoid pain. So I thought. I imagined. I played with possibilities. *Hmmm...* what do you do when you want a fresh start? Another divine download arrived. Pack up kids, we are moving to Alberta!

Within three weeks of my 'awakening,' my request to be released from my work contract was granted, a 'For Sale' sign was in the front yard and I drove to Alberta to find my future. It was July 2 and I absolutely knew that we would be in Alberta for my kids to start school. I just didn't know where or how.

Not knowing anyone in Alberta, a cold-call provided a list of people to contact and I began just showing up and asking for help. I was real, vulnerable and genuine and I received amazing support. On my 16th drop-in visit, I was led to my 'how' in the form of a contract no one knew existed, in an industry I had never worked in, for the income I was seeking, in the community I had hoped to call home.

We arrived in Alberta the day before school started (of course!) and I quickly realized I had value to offer. I authentically showed up every day and made real connections with people. I felt appreciated. I made decisions for me. Life was good.

I was so mesmerized by the beautiful Rocky Mountains that I slowly began neglecting the relationship with myself. Life, however, had other plans, and after a few 'bumps' occurred to remind me that what is outside of me reflects what is inside of me, my self-discovery resumed.

I learned that children of alcoholics often believe their feelings are not important. They do not feel safe to be themselves and 'perfectionism' is a normal side effect. I uncovered and released hidden fears and limiting beliefs. My life became more meaningful. I learned to welcome my emotions and express them in healthy ways. My life felt real.

I no longer show up as the ever-changing chameleon. My journey is now an adventure of self-discovery as I am guided the light of who I truly am, each and every day.

I belong. I AM.

ABOUT DARLIS-KEILY IRELAND

A curious, creative visionary with a playful twinkle in her eye and a heart-warming smile, Darlis-Keily Ireland's genuine approach when speaking, facilitating, and mentoring makes people feel seen, understood, and empowered.

In 20+ years working with businesses, organizations, and rural communities, plus her own personal experience, she has witnessed how higher levels of success are reached when offerings, actions, and messages are delivered with authenticity rather than with salesy marketing.

Frustrated with cookie-cutter programs and techniques that leave people feeling overwhelmed and confused about how to grow their business, Darlis-Keily decided to use her uncanny ability for 'connecting the dots' to guide heart-preneurs into alignment with their business.

By understanding their personal brand, ideal client, transformation provided, and other individualized information, her clients share the right message with the right people in a way that is authentic to who they are, who they serve and how they serve them.

www.DarlisKeilyIreland.com
www.facebook.com/DarlisKeily

Talk About It: Be Prepared, Not Scared

By Lorna Selig

Occasionally a woman makes you realize you need to pay attention. You need to plan. Personal safety is a worry for a lot of women, but most of us never realize we should have a plan. Lorna decided she would come to the rescue, not only for herself, but for many women and children. You've also got to love a woman that gives you the opportunity to kick a man in the groin as part of her curriculum.

I FIND IT remarkable that people spend more time thinking about a new vehicle purchase than they do thinking about and planning for their own or their family's personal safety and protection. Much visualizing, research, and test-driving goes into the purchase of a vehicle, but not as much effort goes into planning for our own safety.

What if we did spend time planning for our personal safety — thinking about, visualizing, and 'test driving' a *Safety Plan*? It could save your life, or certainly prevent a traumatic experience that would likely change your life.

Imagine this scenario: you are leaving work late one evening and you step outside to walk to your vehicle. It's dark and chilly and as you bundle up against the cool air, you are grabbed from behind. As you are crashing to the sidewalk, you realize the danger you are in. This guy doesn't want your purse or your cell phone, he wants *you*. What are you going to do?

If we had spent a bit of time thinking about and planning for a situation like the one above, we could have developed a *Safety Plan* that would have included: screaming, fighting back, and running for help. Unfortunately, for many of us, we haven't considered what we would do in the event of a personal attack. Without a plan, we would likely 'freeze.'

Statistics show that females are more likely to be victims of assault. However, the numbers for male victims are significant as well and it is likely that assaults on males are not always reported. Statistics also show that perpetrators are usually known to the victim which dispels the 'Stranger Danger' myth.

Many of us have stories of assault or exposure to unwanted advances or sexualized behaviour. My first traumatic experience was when I was about 11 years old. Walking home from school, I heard a knocking on a window of a house that I was passing. I looked up to see a male masturbating in the window. The fear and disbelief that swelled up in my belly and chest was one of my first real experiences of that instinctual response to fear and danger. I ran as fast as I could, all the way home. But I never told anyone. And then again, when I was almost 17, at a party, where I had been drinking too much, I was grabbed and forced into the back seat of a vehicle. With hands grabbing at me, and the weight of his body on top of me, I somehow managed to get my feet up to kick him off me and escape out the other door. I straightened myself out and walked back to the party, and I never told anyone! When I was about 25, I had another experience with a restaurant owner who invited me into his office under the guise of paying a parking ticket. He closed the door, stood in front of it and said, "I know what you really want," and he started to remove his suit jacket. I managed to get past him and out of the building, scared, shocked, and in disbelief. This time, I told my boyfriend, who shook his head and asked what I was wearing, and why I went there alone. Again, I was shocked and couldn't quite believe what I had heard or that he had questioned my judgment.

My stories are so similar to many I have heard over the course of my work with families and individuals — people finding themselves in situations where they feel powerless, taken advantage of and victimized in some way. They report that 'suddenly' they found themselves in scary and fearful situations and had no plan for what to do next.

In 2006, I was privileged to see a children's personal safety presentation in my son's school that offered a solution to these victimization situations. I was so impressed with the content of the session, that I reached out to the owner of the company and became involved in teaching safety training and self-defence classes to children and teens. The framework of this curriculum became my personal philosophy — to talk about the importance of personal safety and learn the basic skills to protect yourself. Then, to practice, visualize, and rehearse these skills as a family, thereby creating a *Safety Plan*.

I am often asked about my thoughts on why assault seems to continue and what can be done to stop it. My response is that we need to look at assault prevention in much the same way that we look at car accident prevention. We may not be able to stop assaults from happening, and we may not be able to stop car accidents from happening, but we can put the preventative and preparatory measures in place to reduce incidents and minimize effects. While driving, we wear seat belts, we drive defensively, we reduce distractions and we are in a constant state of awareness of pending dangers. We cannot always predict the state of another driver, nor can we control their actions, but if we have our driving safety plan in place, we can minimize our risk. In much the same way, we can reduce our risk of assault, and we can implement our personal *Safety Plan*. We can be aware, we can avoid areas of potential danger and remove ourselves from uncomfortable situations, and we can have our keys ready to open the car door or to use in defense. We may not be able to predict the behaviour of someone else, nor can we control their actions, but we can protect ourselves to reduce our risk. And if a situation turns frightening or threatening, we know to scream, fight back, and run for help.

I believe that we can change the number of assault incidents by creating a groundswell of thought change within families and our communities. We need to teach our children about respectful, compassionate and responsible behaviour. We must talk with them about what to do if others are not acting with respect toward them, or if they see someone else being violated. These conversations need to happen in an ongoing fashion within families; even children as young as three can participate. Make personal safety and respectful behaviour part of a daily dialogue much the same way that we discuss what our plans are for the evening or what we will be having for dinner. Discussions with children must include ways that they can protect themselves, that no one has the right to violate their body, nor should they violate another's, and that a young child should not be required to participate in the disrespectful behaviour of a person older than them. Remind children that it is not their job to fix an adult problem (like finding a lost pet), and they do not need to hug or sit near someone that makes them feel uncomfortable. Children's sense of danger and their instinctual response is very finely tuned. They know when they feel fear, and we, as adults, need to encourage them to respond to it by leaving that situation and seeking help from an adult they trust. Even if they cannot prove it, their instinct is never wrong.

Giving children information about protecting themselves will empower them and increase their confidence. It will not scare them. Think about the fire drills that are taught in schools and your place of work. These drills are a preventative procedure that has been part of school and office policy for many years. Children participate in fire drills from their first year in school right through to their final graduation. They know the plan because it has been taught and repeated regularly. Even if there is never a fire in the school, children know what to do if there was. They are not in fear of a school fire, they are simply prepared. A **Safety Plan** works the same way. When children have an opportunity to talk about ways to stay safe, they can be prepared, not scared, and they know what to do if they are ever in danger.

Studies show that when people participate in some kind of self-defence or resistance training, they are more likely to avoid or fend off a personal attack in the future. Retention rates are tremendously high for recalling the skills and strategies for escaping a determined predator, especially when the training includes actual hands-on practice. Self-defence training for children through to seniors is one of the best ways to learn the skills and hands-on strategies that shape an effective and usable **Safety Plan**.

An assault or attack is a traumatic and scary event that hopefully you or your loved ones will never have to experience, but being prepared will help to avoid or thwart a threatening situation. Learn and practice self-protection with your family members so that the **Safety Plan** is rehearsed and ready to go if need be. Make **Safety Plans** part of your regular family conversations... be prepared, not scared.

About Lorna Selig

Lorna Selig has been part of the Calgary (Canada) Family and Community Social Services Sector for many years. Her passion for emotional safety and wellness in children and teens has evolved into her Personal Safety Training Company, Safe4Life... More Than Self Defense. Sharing this personal safety information is her life's mission, recoagnizing that family education and conversation is the best way to reduce the incidence and statistics of assault and victimization.

Look for her new family activity and information book "The SafeGuards" on her website: www.safe4life.ca

www.facebook.com/Safe4Life.ca
www.twitter.com/Safe4LifeDotCa

Never Give Up: My Journey with Sonny

By Kelly Kay

Kelly was gifted with a 6th sense I like to call her "horse sense." Not only does she work and play with these mysterious beings, she understands them, talks to them, and even uses their gifts to heal people. Enjoy this intriguing friendship and, I promise, you too will fall in love with Sonny and will be in awe of this strong, compassionate woman.

Have you ever seen the potential in someone even when others didn't? That something, that is in some way a reflection of yourself? When your inner voice tells you to believe in them because that is all that they need to shine and become?

I have had the privilege of being around horses for most of my life and my experiences with them have helped me to trust in myself and to *really* listen not only with my ears but also with my heart.

My parents bought our first pony when I was five years old. I learned very quickly that the horses would mirror me. If I was anxious, they would become anxious. If I was sad, they would be soft and quiet. If I moved too quickly and ran around, they became jumpy. They didn't care what I looked like, only who I was being.

Horses have been the one constant in my life. They have been my compassionate healers. When I went through the grief of losing my dad, my best friend and my sister-in-law, they were always there, unconditionally by my side supporting me, their manes wet from my tears. When I went through my divorce and subsequent transformation, they were still there, humbling me and reminding me to keep it real.

I want to share Sonny's story as he has been one of my greatest teachers thus far.

I first met him when I moved my horses to a boarding facility in 2004.

He was a tall, gangly, dark-coloured colt. In fact, he was rather homely, but with this goofy and sociable charm. At the age of two, he became very ill and almost died. He lost so much weight he literally became a walking skeleton. It was a long recovery, but he pulled through. He always had his head over the fence so I would stop to pet him whenever I walked by. We became buddies as he slowly regained his health and I rather liked him despite his rough appearance.

Due to circumstances, I ended up managing the facility and in essence, all of the owner's horses were in my care, Sonny included. He was still a very social guy, but incredibly pushy and difficult to handle.

I couldn't explain it but there was something that truly endeared him to me. His owner wanted me to "get rid of him." She felt he had suffered brain damage from his illness. There was no way I could sell him to anyone in good conscience as he was somewhat dangerous to handle. He would stand tied in the barn and randomly kick out at the walls. No matter how much he was disciplined, he continued to do it.

He was sent out for training as a four-year-old and when he came home, I went to saddle him and he acted like he had never seen one before, hunching his back and literally trembling as I placed it on his back. The poor guy was absolutely terrified. I asked one of the young experienced riders at the barn to begin working with him as I felt that he needed a lot of attention.

She tried to work with him, but he was completely uncooperative and she gave up after only a few sessions. Needless to say, I sighed and looked at him, and said, "Looks like it's you and me, kid." I wasn't ready to give up on him and write him off quite yet. So, we began our journey.

On the first day, I decided to observe him while he was on his own in the arena. I turned him loose with a halter and rope dangling to teach him how to get over the fear of having something tangled around his legs. It is something that I do with all young horses and although he wasn't a baby, I felt that it was something that he needed to learn regardless.

He was less than pleased! I watched him have a meltdown as he kept stepping on his rope in mid-stride. I just smiled and continued to quietly watch him through the window. What happened next amazed me. There was a jump standard in the middle of the arena and he managed to wind his rope around it and get all tangled up. I thought for sure he would explode. Instead, he turned his ears sideways like a donkey (I learned that this was his thinking pose) and I watched him calmly and carefully extricate himself from his predicament. He finally revealed a little glimpse of what he was made of and my hope for him grew immensely. I realized in that moment he was something special. I already knew that he was a non-conformist; that he was somewhat immature for his age, yet in so many other ways he was ahead of his herd mates.

He was complex and didn't learn in the same way that other horses did. I knew that I had to think outside the box with him. It wasn't going to be easy, but he was worth it. He was very big and strong and I knew that I would never win any arguments with him. I had to pick my battles as he had so many issues. If he was tied in the arena, he would throw himself over backwards. If he was tied in the barn aisle, he would stand patiently for hours. So, I chose not to tie him in the arena. It was far more important that he stood tied in the barn and I didn't want to mess that up.

I have never considered myself a horse trainer. And yes, many horse people would laugh or ridicule me for the methods that I used. I received a lot of advice on how to "force" him to do things and for the first time in my life I stood strong and said, "No. I'll do this my way." I knew that he had the potential to kill someone if they handled him wrong.

I had to exercise extreme patience with him. On numerous occasions, I had to swallow my fear. In fact, one day I decided it was time to get on his back. I was terrified as I took a deep breath, stood on the mounting block and swung a leg over. He felt like he was ready to explode at any given moment and for the next several rides it was the same thing. There were times that he planted me in the dirt and during those times I learned to be assertive and work him hard on the ground until he would take a deep breath and look at me as if to say, "Okay, fine. Let's do it your way." I would get back on and he would be a meek little angel.

My consistent rule with every session was that it had to end on a positive note, no matter how small.

No matter what he did, I refused to give up on him. Every time he did something right, I would praise the heck out of him. He continued to reveal his potential with each passing day. We formed such a strong connection that I knew he needed to be mine so I offered the owner a thousand dollars for him and he joined my herd.

He began to blossom, growing into a gorgeous, tall horse, his dark coat slowly turning grey just like his sire. Today the gangly, weird-looking colt is now a tall, magnificent looking horse with so much presence. He has become my main riding horse and I trust him implicitly to look after me. He always keeps me on my toes. He doesn't cut me any slack, and on the days that I am distracted or my energy is off he won't let me catch him.

Sonny and I had the privilege of riding with Buck Brannaman in November of 2015. It was the fulfillment of a dream and Sonny was an absolute gentleman during the whole three-day clinic. I was so proud of how far we had come as I sat astride him, completely relaxed with a little smile on my face, even though other horses were bolting and spooking around him.

This guy has taught me so many lessons. He taught me to never give up and to pick my battles. From him, I learned to look beyond outward appearances. He taught me about facing my fear and trusting my gut. He taught me to take a deep breath and become still when frustration began to overwhelm me. Most of all he taught me to believe in myself.

Recently Sonny and I have embarked on a new journey. He is my equine partner, healing people who have suffered trauma and grief. I am in awe of his patience, intuition, and compassion. Many times, I look to him for answers because he has such a strong ability to read people. He is my partner, my guide, my friend.

When I think back to how our journey began and where we are today I just smile because I listened to my inner voice for once. We have come full circle.

ABOUT KELLY KAY

Kelly Kay is a Life Coach, Equine Assisted Learning Facilitator, Equine Consultant, Blogger and Reiki Master who is passionate about inspiring her clients to recognize their power as the author of their own story. Through her own experience, she has created a purpose-driven, heart-centred coaching practice that is always inspiring and never feels like work. She is the proud mother of two brilliant young adults and the honorary human member of her herd of six brilliant equine teachers. Kelly also enjoys sharing the magic of horses and their lessons with her clients.

She strongly believes that we all need to lighten up and laugh sometimes. Her signature hashtag is #Live Like You Mean It. Her goal is to inspire others to believe in themselves, to embrace their imperfections, and to take charge of their lives. "We have much to learn from each other, so why not embrace the power of community and support each other as we walk our paths. Together we can move mountains!"

Kelly lives in the scenic and vibrant community of Okotoks, Alberta.

www.kellykaycoaching.com
www.linkedin.com/in/kellykaycoaching
www.facebook.com/Kelly-Kay-Coach-1457764744552995

From Tragic to Magic

By Harriet Tinka, BBA, CPA, CMA, CCF

Powerful, beautiful, mesmerizing... This young woman's story is an incredible, heart-wrenching rollercoaster ride that ends in the most beautiful place possible. She was born with her physical beauty but her inner beauty grew from a horrible manure no woman should have to step in. Her experience will help countless young ladies.

THIS IS A story about learning to love yourself after a traumatic experience.

I stood by the window in the hospital. I had been hobbling on crutches. My mind was distracted with regret and bitterness as the hours passed like minutes. Time had lost its meaning. My movements communicated a loss of self-control and awareness. It was difficult for me to own my story. I preferred running away from it.

I glanced up and down the empty corridor with the same doors and fixtures I had known for the last three months. Behind the doors that lined the corridor lay the ill, broken, and disfigured. The hospital had a mild disinfectant smell. A tall nurse walked by weakly whistling in an attempt to find energy. Her hair was tied back and her eyes were bloodshot from tiredness and troublesome patients. A squeaky noise caught my attention. It was coming from a wheelchair being pushed by an overjoyed eight-year-old girl.

"Hi, what's your name?" she asked attentively.

I felt irritated. At the hospital, I preferred being around people who were solemn and sad so that I could wallow in misery. This cheerful little girl didn't fit into the environment.

"My name is Harriet," I answered impatiently.

"Cool, I am Amber. Why are you here?" She asked interestedly.

"I am here for rehab for my legs," I answered angrily.

"What happened to your legs?" She asked inquisitively.

Flashback to My Trauma

Let's rewind to the past. I was a young teen 5'8" at 110 pounds living the life of a runaway model. I was driven and understood perseverance. It was hard work and not as glamourous as it's portrayed on camera. It was about starvation, workouts, harsh criticism, magazine photoshoots, runaway shows, and midnight fittings. The perks were travelling around the world and experiencing other cultures. I ended that phase of my life and decided to go back to school for a formal education.

My life as a student at the University of Calgary was hectic. My family lived three hours away. Though outwardly I was popular and fit in, on the inside I felt alone and vulnerable. I knew my social limits and was authentic in making friends. Martin was a student I'd met on campus and we became very close. He was extremely charming and clever. But, he was also a manipulative, hypertensive, lonely, pathological liar. Jealousy arose in Martin when I spent time with my fellow students. I never suspected that he could be hatching a plan to harm me, but I sensed a need to keep my distance. Martin became infuriated when I began to avoid him and he became aggressive and relentless in his desire to stay close to me. His obsession became frightening and I obtained a restraining order.

One evening, I stayed late at the university to work on a school project. After a few hours passed, I wrapped things up, and walked back to my apartment building alone. I pressed the elevator button, the doors opened and there he was. Martin had managed to walk into my secured building. I was frozen with fear. Martin pulled a large butcher's knife from his jacket and pulled me into the elevator. Seconds later, I could hear voices coming from the hallway. In a panic, he took the sharp knife and pressed it into my neck to silence me. I was terrified in that moment. I had no doubt that he was going to kill me. He pushed me against the wall, pulled me by the waist close to his body and said, "You know I am the only one who could ever love you unconditionally." He then cut deep into my right hand middle finger. I was in shock as blood poured from my fingers onto the elevator's floor. I tried to scream but he covered my mouth and dragged me by my hair outside.

He slammed my head onto the car as he pushed me inside. My head and fingers were throbbing with pain. He swore loudly at me as he drove recklessly into a nearby car dealership. He stopped, got out of the car, grabbed a baseball bat from the back seat, and proceeded to smash windshields. Martin returned to the driver's seat of his car, looked at me with animosity in his eyes and said, "if you don't listen to me from now on, you'll see." I was panic-stricken. He drove to an isolated area where he saw a phone booth, ordered me to call my family to bid them farewell as it would be the last time they would ever hear from me. I felt shame and sadness. He was ripping my self-esteem to shreds. I rejected his request. In anger, he told me, "I have a rope, a knife, gasoline, and a gun. I am going to tie your body with the rope, cut you into pieces, and burn your body. Nobody will ever find you. Now, go call them." Again, I rejected his request. He took the large butcher's knife he had used to cut my finger and stabbed me twice in my left thigh. I screamed from the excruciating pain as blood splattered the windshield and I lost consciousness.

I woke up in the hospital emergency ward after the doctor had stabilized my injuries. The local media team was in the waiting room. The police and my father were at my bedside. My father drove for three hours that night to be with me. He felt powerless as he stood by my side. Who knew I would become a victim of domestic violence? I was shamed for my family because of what had happened to me. It was, all *my* fault.

My Source of Inspiration

I was in the hospital learning to walk again and slowly beginning to use my badly damaged fingers. My abuser only served three months in jail. I fell into depression, cried constantly, and contemplated ending my life. I did not see the world as a safe place anymore.

Seeing no other way to end my mental agony, I bought a bottle of sleeping pills and was determined to end my life. I gulped them down, wrote my family a goodbye note, and went to bed hoping to end my trauma. Just my luck, I woke up feeling disoriented, dizzy, nauseated, but mostly disappointed that my plan to end my suffering had failed.

* * *

Here sat Amber, in a wheelchair, filled with life, asking why I was in rehabilitation. She shared her tragic story. A drunk driver had caused an accident that resulted in the loss of her entire family. She was confined to a wheelchair for the rest of her life. She was motherless, fatherless, and homeless. Yet amidst all this tragedy she exuded happiness. I asked her how she could be so happy when she had been dealt so much pain. Amber moved close to me and whispered, "Move forward and use your pain to inspire others." At that moment, l knew my suffering was insignificant compared to Amber's story. Her story was the catalyst for my turning point. I realized I am lucky to be alive!

My life journey exemplified three corners of a triangle: model, student, and daughter. Each side of the triangle builds on the other to generate hope, healing and forgiveness. I reflected back on my days as a model. During those years, I saw firsthand the damaging effects that the modeling industry's unrealistic beauty standards can have on young girls. True beauty in that world is unattainable. I decided to recalibrate my life and learn to refocus inwardly on being a better person. I stopped criticizing my flaws and behaved as a role model by being kind, honest, and genuine.

The New Empowered Me

The trauma I experienced taught me that one cannot expect a perfect life but must appreciate moments of beauty and perfection that will be interspersed among dull moments and, at times, tragedy. Amber's inspirational words were a call to action. I was to start loving myself unconditionally and inspire others along the way. I wanted to be a social entrepreneur. Some new entrepreneurs start with an idea or product and then target a relevant market. I did some research in my community to ensure l had a thorough understanding of what existed already, what worked, and what was possible. I then created a community resource map and formed my business called *Empowered Me* with the slogan *"I Believe in Me Because..."* ™. *Empowered Me* is based on building self-esteem, be it from cognitive performance or social interaction. I created this business because of my experiences and my emotional connection with Amber.

A person's self-esteem is negatively impacted after trauma or after years of being in a negative environment. It becomes difficult to learn how to love yourself. One path to self-love is learning to recover from the damage we suffered in our past and how to rise above adversity.

I use a treasure box as a metaphor to explain the components of self-esteem. The three keys I offer my participants to help them open their personal treasure box include:

- *Feeling of belonging*
- *Sense of accomplishment*
- *Sentiment of appreciation*

Having gratitude is a step towards building a strong self-esteem. I keep a journal to capture life's daily grateful moments. I have learned to appreciate how even small events change my personal vibration and create more goodness in my life. With the help of my life triangle, I can now own my story and be compassionate with myself. I describe my life as a journey from tragic to magic.

About Harriet Tinka, BBA, CPA, CMA, CCP

Harriet Tinka is a motivational speaker, life coach, blogger, youth supporter, passion-fueled entrepreneur, and an all-round life enthusiast. Her passion and deepest desire in life is to help empower people of all ages to let go of their limitations and fears so that they can become the best version of themselves. Her clients, who range from age ten and up, want to discover a healthy perception of themselves and strengthen their relationships so that they can feel strong, whole, and safe. Harriet focuses on running life-changing workshops and retreats, speaking in schools, writing inspiring blogs, giving motivational talks to her *Empowered Me* family, and guiding her clients to live the most empowered life possible. She measures her success by how many people she empowers.

www.facebook.com/EmpoweredMeYEG
www.empoweredme.ca

Life on the Edge

By Brynda Roche

Passionate and full of life and laughter, Brynda is always up to a challenge. Being one of my most dedicated Directors, I know I can always count on her. Always looking for ways to improve her life and others, she inspires many women to be all they can be, at times even nudging them, myself included, over the edge.

Brigitte

> *"Come to the edge, he said. We are afraid, they said.*
> *Come to the edge, he said. They came to the edge,*
> *He pushed them and they flew.*
> *Come to the edge, Life said. They said: We are afraid.*
> *Come to the edge, Life said. They came.*
> *It pushed them... And they flew."*
> — GUILLAUME APOLLINAIRE

*I*T SHOULD HAVE been an exciting moment. Instead, I crouched frozen with crippling fear. What was I doing here 3,500 feet above the earth in a pee-wee jump-plane that barely held four people including the pilot? Oh my God, I am going to die! Whose idea was this anyway? I am going to kill them! Oh wait... it was mine. What was I thinking?

As the instructor beckoned me to **The Edge**, the screams inside my head and the indescribable adrenaline surging through my body froze every muscle, every cell, and I was immobilized for what seemed to have been an eternity. He continued to anxiously summon me to the door as we were approaching the point of no return. Knowing I was left with just seconds to decide to jump or return to the ground feeling like a failure, I realized my decision could change the whole course of my life in many ways.

Minutes before, I had witnessed my son and sister dropping out of sight and now it was my turn to leave my secure corner behind the pilot and be "thrown" out into the wild blue yonder — and plummet fiercely to the earth below. I was certain they would be dead when I got down there, if I survived.

Frantically, I began looking deep inside my soul for any sliver of courage as I pleaded with God to jump with me. I inched my way to the door and suddenly something rose up from the depths of my soul. All other thoughts vanished and giving myself that internal terrified PUSH, I screamed...

"GO TO THE EDGE BRYNDA! GO TO THE EDGE — NOW!!!!!"

As I reflect back to places and times where life took me to **The Edge**, I realize I really didn't know what that had meant. My first recollection appeared at eight years old when my mother left my father in a frenzied hurry in the middle of a cold winter night, stuffing belongings and five children into a vehicle that would transport us from security to the unknown.

At a time where it was not as acceptable to be a single mother — let alone one with five children — my mother bestowed upon me the responsibility of becoming the caregiver of my siblings at a very young age while she worked. Years later, she had her sixth child and once again I became the surrogate mother to this infant.

My childhood vanished into a sea of responsibility. Many times, I stood on **The Edge** not knowing what to do but having to make adult decisions.

I craved play. I craved the innocent freedom of being a child. I became introverted and shy being locked into a world I had no business being in yet. I yearned for safety and security.

As the years progressed, I chose careers and relationships that would bring me what I thirsted for, or so I believed. For years I led a life of control: the perfect house, immaculate, everything in order, structured, controlled. I sheltered my personal life from those whom I did not know. I was afraid of being imperfect and judged.

I was not "flying" and I didn't know why. I became a voracious student of life. I struggled as I searched for meaning and purpose. I felt restrained and restricted.

A tipping point came for me when my mother unfortunately passed away in her early fifties. Once again, I found myself caring for my siblings, guiding them through the tragic loss of not only our mother but also the recent suicide of one of my twin brothers.

As we held our 24/7 vigil in the Vancouver Cancer Hospital, I became acutely aware of what was *not* important in life and I began my quest to discover what *was*. Something inside me yearned to be free, to soar.

Daily, I quietly cried. "My wings are in there — I am an eagle! I am an eagle! I am an eagle! I am not a duck!" Confused, I paddled in the muddy waters of uncertainty, limiting beliefs, fear, the past, and the childhood I never knew.

Allow me to explain. I love to use the analogy of ducks and eagles when I work with my team and my clients as a form of encouragement.

I love ducks! Ducks are good. They have the ability to fly and are amazing followers. But they live a somewhat limited life. They *paddle-paddle-paddle* through life often times in murky waters and stay within the confines of their ponds, unaware of the vast adventures awaiting them. *Preen-Paddle-Follow.* Same thing, day after day, year after year, and they're okay with that. *I am not okay with that.*

I have been blessed to witness eagles soaring at high altitudes, falling confidently away from the edges of the cliffs. I watched them push past their comfort zones, flying high above the ponds and rivers and knowing their incredible vision allows them to view the glory of the world below.

Eagles inspire me. What intrigues me most is that in the midst of a storm the eagle spreads its mighty wings towards the stormy winds and uses the current to soar to greater heights. Life holds no limits! *I am okay with this.*

It took a while, a few bumps and bruises, and some hard knocks, nonetheless, I decided to explore life in the ways the eagle does.

Now let me to talk to you about **The Edge** and its significance to me.

I discovered that **The Edge** is the place where we stand in decision towards change. On one side is life as it is and on the other side is where new experiences and possibilities begin. It is a place to stand still, listen to our inner wisdom, allow ourselves to be challenged and then move towards our potential, to transform and to fly. It's a place where we can release our fear, the fear that stops us from being all we are meant to be and allow the doors of possibility to open. A place to choose to shift our energy and our circumstances, a place to push off and soar!

The Edge presented itself to me many times throughout my life. Times when I skydived, rode a motorbike through steep mountains, went whitewater rafting, jumped off a two-storey boat in Bermuda (Did I tell you I am deathly afraid of water?), rappelled off 29 stories in a bird costume using immense trust as I stepped up on that ledge backwards and walked the brave journey down the wall.

The Edge also existed in my career choices and volunteer work, including: hairstyling, special needs associate, IT manager, successful network marketing leader, Choices Coach, True Colors Facilitator, and Discover Your Sacred Gifts Guide. Looking back, I can clearly see many times where I stood on that edge, with fear and doubt, uncertain if I was capable. But I stepped off anyway.

And I am forever grateful I did. It allowed me to encounter life's brilliancy and learn many lessons along the way. Each defining experience, whether delightful or devastating, taught me what truly was important in life and just how precious it is. I share with you a few of those lessons:

- Count your blessings big and small.
- Put on Different Glasses. Look for the beauty in all situations.
- Change your state, change your energy, change your mindset.
- Let go of the past. Release toxic people and situations that keep you paddling in the murky waters, limiting your potential.
- Adopt a motto: Not my zoo, not my monkeys.
- Play with the innocence of a child. Wear piggy-tails and face paint in public. Dance whenever and wherever. Be Young at Heart.

- Be courageous and brave and cherish your fears. Face them head on and push towards the splendor life has to offer. Trust yourself.
- Eat-Crunch-Taste-Smell all the delicious adventures and moments life presents daily.
- Don't waste time. Life is short. Live your dreams.
- Treasure the moments with all people before you. Look at each one as a gift. Seek to untie their ribbons to experience their magnificence. Be their cheerleader!
- Continue to rely on your deepest beliefs and trust that, "With God all things are possible."
- Embrace your gifts and the potential bestowed upon you and give them back to the world with exuberance and excellence.
- Know that deep within you is an eagle and you can soar to great heights. The freedom to fly really is possible. It's your choice.
- Visit **The Edge** frequently! Don't worry about the What Ifs — JUST DO IT!
- Lastly, believe you are Unstoppable.

Now, you'll have to excuse me... I suddenly have a burning desire to soar!

ABOUT BRYNDA ROCHE

Brynda Roche has worn many hats throughout her career. Ranging from a hairdresser, bank representative, special needs associate, network administrator, computer instructor, Choices Coach, Divorce Care for Kids facilitator, Rainbows Group facilitator to her current career as a successful antiaging specialist and entrepreneur, a True Colors facilitator, and Sacred Gifts guide.

Brynda's mission is to help others enhance the way they live, work, communicate and interact with those around them. She specifically helps others discover their personality style and their sacred gifts as well as to live healthier, younger, and more vibrant lives. Brynda has an extreme passion for inspiring and empowering others to soar to the heights of their God-given potential and discover who they truly are meant to be, to achieve their heart desires and to live a life of purpose and fulfillment.

www.facebook.com/bryndaroche
www.twitter.com/bryndaroche
www.dynamicyou.nsproducts.com

Hay Sister!
What Will You Become?

By Allison Hay

Sisterhood can be a tricky portfolio to manage, but Allison and Lynda have it figured out. Two very different souls, from very different perspectives, they have negotiated a balanced relationship. They elevate, encourage and push each other to be more at work and at play. From investment to running marathons to wine drinking, they have learned to respect, embrace, and love their differences.

GROWING UP FEMALE in the 70's was fantastic. We were the first generation of girls to have the freedom to become anything we wanted. That may not sound like any big deal now, or maybe it does. It was a heady concept as a young girl, to be encouraged to think beyond the traditional female roles of secretary or nurse or to work until you got married and had children. Now, suddenly, we were encouraged to go to University, to dream, and to conquer. It was a little intimidating to be able to choose from everything and then ask yourself, "What do I want to be when I grow up?" Having a mother who worked outside of the home and an artist father who worked from the basement was helpful. We didn't realize that we were enjoying an untraditional upbringing, it was just home.

Lynda and I both knew that when we grew up, we wanted to be able to take care of ourselves and be financially independent. When I reflect back on our dreams and goals as young girls, I realize now that we were amid changing times for women. Nevertheless, from that common goal, my sister Lynda and I took off in opposite directions. Lynda knew at the age of 13 that she would be a stockbroker. She would be married, and she would be successful, and enjoy all the trappings of that success.

She had a plan, a goal, and off she went. As for me, I knew that I wanted to have my own place and I wanted to have a dog. Anything else was as tangible as smoke.

Dad said something to me at that time that has served me well all through my life. He said, "Kid, whatever success you have in your life, you'll fall into, so, don't worry so much about it." Those words were very reassuring to me and set the tone for the next 15 years of my life. Looking back, I recall watching with a bit of envy and a lot of bemusement as Lynda planned her way through the same 15 years. I'm sure that she had a similar feeling of wonder and eye-rolling as I attempted to figure out where I belonged.

Lynda was the youngest female broker ever hired at Merrill Lynch Canada in 1986. She persevered and succeeded in a business that is pretty tough, especially for a woman. Lynda was playing the role that she had prepared for since she was 13. She checked everything off her list. Funny thing... wanting what you have can be very different than getting what you want. I had enjoyed success as a hotel and restaurant manager, but was still in search of a 'life'... something that is virtually non-existent in the hospitality business. I had a place of my own and a dog. Hay sister! What happens now?

Almost 17 years ago, two wandering paths collided and we found ourselves agreeing to work together in Lynda's business. So, the free-spirited sister and the conservative sister formed a team and much to our surprise, we discovered that very different paths can lead to the same destination, and very different sisters can see things in a surprisingly similar way.

Sure enough, it was Lynda's turn to be amused as she witnessed the free-spirited, spontaneous being I envisioned as myself, embrace the detail oriented, methodical, *that's not on the list* kinda gal I am. I guess that Dad was correct after all. You fall into your success for the most part, and whatever planning you do, you'll get to where you are supposed to be. Lynda, for her part, did get to her planned destination, only to change the role from the traditional, hard-edged broker to a softer, kinder, don't take yourself so seriously, *I want to play with my dog* kinda gal.

It's interesting to me that you can fight to be one thing your whole life and then end up looking around and thinking, "Hmm, I like where I am, and that's cool. Look how this worked out."

In the business that I am currently in, it's wonderful to meet all sorts of people on various paths. Some are marching with purpose towards a clear destination, some timidly moving towards something, somewhere hidden in smoke. I believe you have to have a plan for life to be able to take care of yourself, because having that foundation gives you the opportunity to then take care of others. That plan can be for a spouse, family, friends, pets, a cause, or a belief. That plan also allows you to be open to the opportunity that comes your way and that's the fun part. When you're on solid footing, you get to veer off into the unknown every now and again and explore that part of you that you might have ignored because it wasn't on the list.

Give yourself permission to go out and discover new talents, new qualities. Those great discoveries don't happen if you're too busy looking at your destination. When Lynda turned 40 (this is where I am able to work in the fact that Lynda is 4 years older than me), I signed us up for our first marathon run! I know what you're thinking. *What a lovely gift. How thoughtful.* It was, really. I did it for a couple of reasons: first, our bodies (mine especially) were experiencing a response to gravity that dramatically reminded me of those modern art sculptures where body parts are shifted around for artistic effect. Not attractive. Also, I knew that Lynda and I are competitive enough with each other that we would do this. So, we did. And since then, we've dragged each other through many different races and it's just what we do now. I don't think that Lynda likes it any better than she did that first time, but we no longer look like modern art either.

Running and playing with our dogs, painting, and even writing this story, I believe, makes us a better team, better advisors, closer sisters, better friends and daughters.

The Hay Sisters have evolved into a people based business that helps all sorts of interesting individuals to establish a foundation. We help them to clear the smoke a little bit and then we get to walk with them towards their destinations. Look at how that worked out? All of the qualities, intentions, and ideas that we had combined to form a business that was known for being pretty hard-edged and product focused, but it is actually now people focused and reflects who Lynda and I are as humans. So, I guess, we didn't become what we wanted; we became what we are.

It's been quite an interesting journey so far, and looking back, I can see where my path has swerved and joined others and then shifted and turned to a new direction. I'm blessed to have so many footprints along my own, especially Lynda's. I know that Lynda still carries a checklist, and I must admit that I have one of my own now, but I still hear Dad's words in my ear, and look forward to exploring some off-road possibilities along the way.

ABOUT ALLISON HAY

Lynda Hay, Allison Hay

Allison and Lynda Hay are close sisters within a small family in Calgary. They are tightly bound to their community and their clients as Investment Advisors. They have worked as a team since 2000 and take great pride in the responsibility they share.

In addition to their business interests, Allison and Lynda Hay are both supporters and enthusiasts of the arts and favourite philanthropic endeavours. As much as they love their work, they love to play and travel as well. The sisters are avid runners and seekers of beaches and palm trees, and ridiculously devoted humans to their respective dogs.

www.facebook.com/profile.php?id=100008727882696

It's A Man's World —Or Is It?

By Jenna Wood

Jenna had not only chosen to work in one of the sexist industries there is, but chose the worst possible position for a female — sports broadcaster. That says a lot about the strength of this busy modern mother of two. Her story reminds us all that the battle is not over yet! We do have what it takes to live in a man's world, even if we're told we don't fit.

*I*T'S FUNNY HOW sometimes when you're in the middle of something really great and unique that you don't really realize how great and unique it is.

When I was only 22 years old, I was co-hosting a province-wide radio sports talk show in Saskatchewan. When I was 23, I was co-host on a morning show on a sports radio station, followed up daily with a one-hour call-in show of my own. I was game-day host for a WHL radio broadcast and working in television part-time for various sports programs as well. Looking back seven years after leaving my broadcasting career, I was doing a lot of really great things and was one of very few females doing them.

Now, in my second career, I am a land agent by trade and a project manager on a day-to-day basis. Once again, I managed to choose the path less travelled by women, without really giving much thought to that particular part of it.

As much as I love my current job and as much as I loved my previous career, upon further reflection, I have faced some very interesting challenges, in large part, just because I am female.

I'll never forget the day I was sexually harassed on the air during my call-in show. I was young and naive and never would have referred to it that way at the time, but looking back, that's exactly what it was. I picked up the call and rather than a comment on the sports topic du jour, all I heard was, "Hey Jenna, will you stick three fingers up my ass while you jerk me off?" Horrified and momentarily stunned, I didn't know what to do. I looked desperately at my producer, who wasn't paying attention at all as I tried to get him to drop the call. I hit and held the drop button, praying that we were on delay. I said something along the lines of, "let's get back to the sports talk" and picked up the next call, just hoping and praying the next caller wouldn't follow suit.

The rest of the show went off without a hitch but the worst part of the whole situation was yet to come when I spoke to my boss about it. What do you think his first question was? I thought he might ask: "Are you ok?" "Is there anything we can do?" or "Would you like us to find the guy and make him pay dearly for hurting you?" Instead, his first question was, "How did that get to air?"

I didn't realize it then, but his response was the start of the end of my career in sports broadcasting. I had always felt I had support from many of my peers. In fact, I know I did because they thought I was good at what I did, and therefore *I belonged*. The only condition to "belonging" was that I didn't ruffle feathers. If I didn't refer to that "unfortunate incident" as sexual harassment and remained a "cool chick" who didn't get upset about things like that, then I fit right in.

And so, I went on like that for a while. I turned the other cheek for many situations that I hope other women in sports will not have to face, never mind ignore. Many of those stories I have never shared, until years later. Even worse, many stories I did share, but I pretended they didn't bother me.

On a daily basis, I received emails from listeners berating me for having the audacity to speak publicly about my love of sports. I managed to resurrect a few old emails and here are some of the best:

Would you just shut up already? If I wanted your opinion on something, I would tune in to a cooking show or the cleaning network. (Aha, I see, "women belong in the kitchen, cooking and cleaning." Now that's original.)

"Y do U think UR the expert on sports? Who died n made U the queen of the lesbian sports teams?" (This person was ahead of the times. Look at all the shorthand and this is before texting became popular!)

Stop talking on the radio and go on TV. If I have to listen to you talk about hockey, I should at least get to stare at your T$%ts while I do it!

Why should I listen to your opinion about sports? Have you ever played professionally? Have you ever won a Stanley Cup? Have you ever won a Grey Cup? Super Bowl? Can you even throw a football? You probably skate like a deer.

These are just a few examples of the emails I received over the course of my career in sports broadcasting. Towards the end, I finally engaged. I snapped. I'd had enough. One day I received an email from a guy who went on and on about how fat and ugly I was and how annoying my voice was. I replied to him in an email saying I was on the radio, so why did it matter if I was fat or ugly? I am certain some people may have described some of the men I worked with at various times as fat or ugly, but did they receive daily emails about it? No, they did not. Wouldn't you know this guy sent me back a picture of a cow wearing a name tag with *my name* written on it! That was the last straw. Not only was the guy a jerk, but he had used his work email account, and he worked for a station sponsor! I took the email to our General Manager and our Sales Manager and told them I thought it would be prudent to let the sponsor know that one of their employees was giving their company a bad name. It took some convincing, but they did. I was told that I would not receive any further contact from this gentleman and if I did, I was not to respond, but was to simply inform the Sales Manager, who would in turn inform the listener's boss. Soon after, I received an email from the listener's personal account. In an expletive-laced tirade, he blasted me for being weak, for going to his boss when he was "just joking around" and called me stupid. I forwarded the email as I had been instructed and never heard from him again.

While I feel that I won that battle, it was another step towards the edge of that career for me. I had been fighting for a long time and I was at a point where I wasn't sure I wanted to fight anymore. I was tired of people assuming I was bad at what I did just because I was a woman. I was sick of people asking me, "do you really like sports?" Anyone who has ever spent ten minutes with me knows I love sports. Somehow, I let them get to me, a little bit at a time and I started to lose my passion for the job I had loved.

Sometimes I wonder what would have happened if I was older when I joined the world of sports broadcasting. If I was already a mother, already a person who is determined to ensure my daughter is never subjected to those same inequalities as I was, would I have fought harder? Would I have been more vocal? Would I have pushed harder and been louder instead of just walking away?

I don't regret walking away because that brought me to a career I love whole-heartedly. I'm in the corporate world now — a world of professionals and business people who are educated and functioning, contributing members of society. So, surely these types of things don't happen anymore, *do they*?

Actually, they do. I'm lucky that I work with some of the best guys in the industry who are also supportive and open to having a woman in what was traditionally a "man's role." However, outside the confines of my comfy little office, there are things I do notice.

Many people assume I'm an administrator and not an agent. I don't really care, because both are very important roles and one could not be done without the other, but it bothers me that they see a woman and assume she has taken a certain path to be where she is.

When I am out in the field or even at some client visits with a male coworker, it is almost always assumed that the male coworker is the boss and I am the "underling", without any consideration of our age or how we are introduced. I think the only thing worse than this is the assumption that I am the wife of the coworker and not actually there for any functional purpose.

In the grand scheme of things, these are small issues. Both sports broadcasting and surface land have come a long way. I believe women are competent, confident and that our communication skills can often set us apart from the pack.

Am I a woman living in a man's world? I guess you could say that. But from my persrpective it's my world I'm living in, and the rest of them are just borrowing space.

ABOUT JENNA WOOD

Ever since she was a girl, Jenna has been interested in "boys" stuff: sports, going to work with Dad, getting dirty and throwing bales on the farm. She's never bought into the traditional roles of men and women and probably never will. Just ask her husband, who often plays single Dad when Jenna travels for work and has mastered the art of not only a ponytail, but a braid and bun. So, what happens when a girl like that grows up and needs a job? She finds herself in male-dominated industries, fighting for equal exposure, equal pay and equal treatment. From a career in sports-broadcasting, right through to the corporate world, Jenna has managed to carve a successful career as a woman in a "man's world."

www.instagram.com/jldub1
www.twitter.com/JLDub10
www.linkedin.com/in/woodjenna
www.facebook.com/jenna.wood.334

Amelia

Amazing Chef, Mother, Teacher and Friend.
A Legacy of Little Life Lessons Worth Sharing.

BY BERNADETTE GERANOZZO

Bernadette is a beautiful, graceful artist that can take you on a true Italian journey with any medium she chooses. The desire to entertain is in her eyes, her dance moves, and most certainly her pen is undeniable. Grab a glass of red wine (Italian of course) and allow Bernadette to take you on the amazing journey of Amelia. I guarantee you will love and be moved by it. Oh, you might also want to have tissues handy.

Brigette

ONCE UPON A time there lived a beautiful young and adventurous girl named Amelia. She was born during the hardships of the Second World War to a humble, country family which lived in Reggio Emilia -the "bread basket" of Italy.

Despite their challenging circumstances, her family recognized Amelia had a strong, capable, and resilient character. They encouraged her to explore her unique and diverse interests. Amelia was a child filled with deep curiosity, intelligence, and fearlessness.

She was blessed with a mother who took the time and patience needed to nurture her little girl's interest in cooking and helped her to: bake bread in the wood-burning stove, create pasta sheets which became lasagna, tortellini and tortelloni, ravioli, cappelletti, cannelloni, as well as many other traditional kinds of pasta that the Emilia-Romagna region is famous for.

A bright student born with the desire to learn and possessing a patient temperament, Amelia began studying to become a doctor. When her mother fell ill, she dutifully left her studies to care for her and her brother and father.

In her mid-twenties, Amelia left Reggio Emilia for the port city of Genova where her sister's family lived. These were happy and fulfilling years. She had her own apartment, a Fiat 500 car, time to enjoy the pleasures of playing with her young niece and nephew, and the freedom to enjoy life along the Ligurian Riveria.

One day, Amelia, accompanied by her sister Anna and Anna's children, went to the local fair. The ever-skeptical Amelia entered the Fortune Teller's caravan with Anna to hear what the future might hold for her.

"You will travel to a far and distant land for love of a man and there you will have a family of your own. It will be difficult — perhaps even heart-breaking for you. The culture and language are not your own but you will make a life for yourself there and you will have influence over the lives of many young children," the Fortune Teller told her.

"That's ridiculous," Amelia said to her sister, Anna. "I'm not getting on a plane to live in a foreign place because of some man. She must be crazy!"

The Fortune Teller, however, was quite right. A few years later, she followed her heart and left everyone in her familiar life to be with a man she hardly knew but deeply loved and went to live in a land where everything was strange and different. She poured her talent and affections into this new life, now filled with the many obligations a small family of two girls and a boy brings.

During their early years at school, Amelia demonstrated determination by taking the local bus the one and a half hours each way for two years to obtain her English Language certification and to graduate with an Early Childhood Development Diploma from the University of Calgary.

This allowed her to secure work at the local daycare facility, which was within easy walking distance of her home. Her intention was to be home each lunch hour to welcome her three children at the table with home-cooked meals and an open heart. She listened attentively to their stories of wonder or woe and offered solutions to the troubles voiced.

Amelia and her husband made sure their children understood a few realities of life at an early age:

Life is not fair.
People do not have equal learning abilities
so you must ALWAYS do your best.
There are Winners and there are Losers —
so if you choose to do less than your best there is always
someone willing to work harder and take your place.

Competition was encouraged and they felt the sooner their children learned the truth about life, the better equipped they would be to succeed. Equipping them also included giving them a series of chores. They learned how to make their beds, hand-wash and dry dishes after dinner, clean the house, care for the family dog, iron, do laundry and much more. By completing these and other tasks they could earn a small allowance which could be saved or spent.

"It doesn't matter how much money you make, what matters most is how much you are able to SAVE!", their father lectured to his children as he handed them their allowance. Other messages included:

School is where you go to learn, so pay attention
to the teacher and do your homework.
It is your duty to help those who may not have your advantages.

Every Sunday the family attended the Italian Catholic Church service where the message regarding respect for authority and honouring one's parents was a favorite theme. For this reason, and the fact that Amelia's husband was by and large a strict father, all the children had a healthy respect for authority.

One afternoon, as they were getting dressed in their Sunday best to drive across town to visit another family's home for dinner, the eldest asked, "Mama, why are you bringing that cake? Is it someone's birthday?"

"No, my dear," Amelia replied, "Even a country bumpkin knows that when you have been invited to dinner you dress for the occasion and you bring a gift. In our case, we are bringing this cake and some of your dad's homemade wine to share — it's just the right thing to do. You would never dream of arriving at anyone's home without some kind of gift for them. It's just not done!"

With that, the family gathered together and piled into the car to visit their friends.

Such fun they had: the parents played cards, the boys and girls played "Hide-and-Seek," then listened to records and danced in the lower level of the house, away from their parents and free to ask the myriad of questions that uninhibited children speak with ease.

All too soon the children were called up to get ready to leave. Amelia was heard saying, "It was really very kind of you to invite us for dinner. Let's have you over for dinner at the end of this month. How does that sound?"

Thus began a tradition of parents having friends' families over for dinner, while the children played games and listened to music, and then their friends returned the favour. Television impeded conversation and was, therefore, turned off in favour of games like Monopoly, Pictionary, Scrabble and the favorite, "Hide-and-Seek."

Amelia's encouragement to help her children find their own sense of style and individuality manifested in teaching the context of what following others could lead to. "So, just because everyone else is jumping off a bridge, you want to go and jump in after them?"

Like many parents, Amelia instilled confidence in her little ones by seeking to make possible for each child that which they desired to try. By allowing them the freedom and encouragement to do/be anything they dreamed of, she bestowed one of the greatest gifts one person can give another — Respect. By respecting that her children knew what they wanted, by uplifting their choices and encouraging them to pursue them, this in turn strengthened their confidence.

Time passed, the children grew into adults and before long everyone had left home to pursue work or studies.

Meanwhile, Amelia's life continued to be an endless stream of giving: to her husband, her co-workers, her neighbours, her adult children and, on rare occasions, to herself.

One cool winter night, just before Christmas, her eldest asked, "Mama, would you come to our performance? I'll be dancing a solo with the guitarist!"

"Yes, of course, that will be wonderful. I'm sure both of us will be happy to be there," as she nodded towards her husband.

The atmosphere in the little theatre was filled with anticipation as the dancers' backstage nervously added final touches to their hair, make-up, and outfits.

The Flamenco guitar ensemble had everyone's attention fixed on the stage and the opening group performance ended with enthusiastic cheers and applause. The show continued with one choreographed piece after another until the final solo performance — the one with her daughter dancing. The audience gazed intently on the stage but in an instant, Amelia slumped beside her husband. "I need an ambulance," she said, "Now!"

From there the world of lights and excitement morphed into a strange, slow motion sequence of events. The paramedics placed Amelia onto the stretcher and raced to the ambulance while the rest of the family rushed to arrive at the hospital just as Amelia was wheeled in. Their father could not face the reality that his wife was suffering a brain aneurysm and suddenly the roles of mother and daughter seemed to switch.

"You know," Amelia said bravely, "I'm not afraid of dying. Many people have died from aneurysm in the brain."

"I'm sure that's true, Mama," said her daughter, "but you will be fine. The doctors are here and they will take care of everything, you'll see. You'll be up and about in no time!"

Amelia was lucid for a full 14 days before ascending to Heaven.

For her family, friends, neighbours and all who knew her, Amelia's passing happened much too soon. No one was prepared. Many realized they had not done enough to thank her for the lasting examples she had provided nor for the many gifts of love she had bestowed. Everyone would miss the blessing of her being, but those who knew her would take from the life she lived many valuable lessons.

May you, dear reader, be inspired to adopt a lesson or two from Amelia on how to act and where to extend kindness, compassion, generosity, and courtesy.

About Bernadette Geronazzo

Over the years, Bernadette Geronazzo has empowered organizations that range from the non-profit to publicly traded companies with specific public and investor relations initiatives.

Corporate leaders from this wide cross-section of business enterprise have trusted her company *In the Public Eye* to provide outside eyes and understanding for their current business challenges. She has helped many to implement creative communication strategies that have enabled them to realize their goals and objectives.

A captivating public speaker and wise leader, Bernadette has had the privilege of holding a variety of Board Member positions, has launched several signature events, has been a newspaper columnist, a radio and even television show host.

As a public relations professional, Bernadette Geronazzo has been recognized by the International Association of Business Communicators with a Gold Quill Award. She has recently been published in a recent book book entitled "Empowering Women Leaders."

www.inthepubliceye.ca

Downstage: When Words Ignite

By Vicki Goodfellow-Duke

The first time I attended Vicki's workshop I was mesmerized and fell in love with public speaking. Her knowledge is undeniable and her love for her craft is contagious. Vicki might be an introvert, but in front of her students she is a rock star! She is a truly gifted teacher and she has changed my life.

FIONA WAS TERRIFIED. Her entire adult life had been spent dodging public speaking commitments, and here she was on the brink of jumping into the fire itself.

Fiona's fear of public speaking was so intense that she had forfeited a wedding ceremony to avoid delivering vows. A successful CEO, Fiona was conveniently busy when asked to train subordinates or chair a meeting. She deferred responsibility to workmates, and no one was the wiser. Eventually, her colleagues became suspicious and she was forced to accept speaking engagements, only to feign illness at the last minute. That was when Fiona called me. Enough was enough.

Fiona is the product of our culture, a culture which, at every turn, appears to demand perfection from us. We worry that we are not good enough or not smart enough. Speaking in front of a group magnifies our insecurities. What if we blank out? What if the audience is bored? And the list goes on.

There is a basic but faulty assumption which presumes that the ability to speak, an adequate vocabulary and expertise in a discipline, are sufficient qualifications for success in public speaking.

According to studies on communication modalities, time spent writing, in a day, averages 9% of daily communication. The average time spent speaking and listening in a 24-hr period, jumps to 75%.[1]

In North American schools, however, from grades 1–12, instructional hours on writing-related activities averages around the 80% mark, while instruction in speech-related activities averages only 3%.[2]

Children are taught to write, but not taught to speak. The absence of instruction is a message itself. If it's not taught, it must be unnecessary. This message is perpetuated beyond school years into adulthood. We are expected to deliver clear, well-organized training sessions and motivational appeals, while being given minimal, sub-par, or no instruction at all in how to do so effectively. Lack of knowledge creates fear and lack of training creates mediocrity.

I am an introvert by nature. I love crowds, parties, and socializing. I love my loud, boisterous classes of college students, and I love my large, high-energy young family. However, after teaching a three-hour class and before going home, admittedly, I need to sit by myself (often in my car) and re-energize. Then I can happily do it all over again.

Because I am an introvert, my parents enrolled me in Speech Arts lessons, a decision which would shape my future career, and to some degree my persona. These lessons gave me the opportunity to perform literature, develop confidence, and to compete. While these experiences afforded many valuable life lessons, as a future *public speaker* they were also detrimental. When memorizing literature, accuracy was essential. I couldn't paraphrase Shakespeare, or Linda Pastan, my favorite poet. Precision makes or breaks a performance. There was immense pressure to be perfect.

Over time, I learned that perfection is not the key to success, neither in speech nor in life. I have learned the best lessons from my students and my coaching clients.

Tom, a civil engineer, hired me to evaluate his prepared speech, which he had delivered many times. He was comfortable with the material and was not the least bit nervous. He wanted to know why, though, shortly

---

1. Walton, D. "Teaching Speaking and Writing" National Center for Literacy. National Council of Teachers of English. Oct 2015. Web. Jan 2017.

2. Ibid.

into every one of his presentations, people seemed to yawn and look out the window, and how, after post-speech discussions with his colleagues, they could hardly recall a single idea he had presented. Within minutes of listening to Tom speak, the problem was clear. In that short period, he had presented six charts, four complex diagrams, and had rattled through such content-heavy material, that my head was spinning.

Dan, a senior level manager in the finance industry, approached me to work with his team. Apparently, he was a professional speaker who had no need for coaching. After working with his team over the course of a few months, Dan began to listen in on our sessions and to ask questions as to why I suggested certain approaches to organizing the material and strongly advised against others. Like many people, he had failed to appreciate the importance of particular psychological factors which must determine the way we frame content.

Is public speaking then, both daunting and difficult? By what measurement can we gauge success? What does an audience want in a public speaker and what does an audience expect from a speech?

In teaching and coaching over the past two decades, the answers to these questions have become clear to me, answers which have been borne out by research in neuroscience, business, and psychology. Audiences expect warmth and competence in a speaker. They crave connection and relationship, and seek information which will improve their lives.

The research and writings of Brené Brown, Ori and Rom Brafmann, among others, have brought to light an essential truth: we like people better when we perceive them as *imperfect.* In a culture where we strive continually to hide our imperfections, this is counter-intuitive. The secret to making connections is vulnerability. We like those who are similar to us and we are astutely aware of our own weaknesses. Connections are forged when we allow the speaking process to be fresh, raw, and in real time, when we show our true selves, when we trust the energy that spontaneity brings.

This is wonderful news for the public speaker. The demand for perfection is an illusion. It was great news for me as I made the transition from performer to public speaker, and it was great news for Fiona who could now share her beautiful, witty, imperfect self with the world.

Audiences have simple expectations from a speech: to recall relevant data, and be able to apply it. While the answer is simple, the application is not.

Cognitive Load Theory teaches us that the human brain, on a functional level, has limitations. Imagine three baskets, which represent your brain's capacity for processing information in a single instance. The first basket contains the load you currently carry with you, all of your concerns, thoughts, worries, desires, etc. (Intrinsic Load)

The second basket is the data, information, visuals, that a speaker will give you during the course of a speech. (Extraneous Load)

In order for the brain to process and incorporate new data from the Extraneous Load, available space is needed in the third basket. (Germane Load) If the Extraneous Load basket overflows with too much data, you experience mental fatigue and have no space for Germane Load. Without brain capacity to relate and apply the information to yourself *during* the speech, you will retain little to nothing.

Remember Tom, the engineer? Tom attempted to cover far too much information. He thought more was better. His audience was continually overwhelmed with data and could not process and retain content.

Knowing how much information to include in a speech is crucial. Knowing how to structure the data is also crucial, particularly when the purpose of the speech is to influence.

While Dan was a talented speaker, he was missing out on opportunities for greater success due to the organization of his material. Once he understood the cognitive processes by which the brain receives and manages information, and the factors which influence decision-making, Dan became a legend in his company and a master of influence.

Before we commit to something new, we all ask ourselves two magical questions: Am I capable? Is it worth it?

Are you capable? Yes. Fiona learned that she was beyond capable, and the same is true for each of us. You are unique, with something precious to offer the world, something no one else can replicate. You have the power to come to know yourself profoundly, to reveal yourself in truth and in passion. Once you have done due diligence in preparation, you are capable of trusting the raw fire of the moment and use your words to ignite change.

Study is the key to proficiency. With knowledge, Tom and Dan transformed their presentations. If you wish to be a great artist, then take classes and observe the masters. Public speaking is no different.

I have taught or coached over six thousand people thus far, and I truly believe that anyone can become a comfortable, confident speaker, and with training and practice, a phenomenal speaker. Most people are simply unaware of the potential and power within themselves, to connect deeply, to inspire and influence.

Is it worth it? I think you know the answer, but permit me. It has truly been an honour for me over the years, to watch young women find their voices and go out into the world and speak out. It has been an honour to witness people from diverse backgrounds sharing their innermost selves and forging unexpected bonds, to see women and men, old and young, extroverts and introverts, speaking from the soul and changing hearts on stages large and small. Yes, my friends, it is worth it.

ABOUT VICKI GOODFELLOW-DUKE

Vicki Goodfellow Duke has had the pleasure of teaching Public Speaking in the Faculty of Business and Communications at Mount Royal University since 1991.

She is passionate about helping people become confident communicators in both their personal and professional lives. Vicki has special interest and expertise in persuasive speaking and rhetoric.

Vicki taught Speech Arts and Drama for The Mount Royal Conservatory from 1990 until 2011. She was a National Examiner for Speech Arts and Drama for The Royal Conservatory of Toronto from 1996 to 2001, and has given workshops and adjudicated festivals across Canada.

Vicki holds a Bachelor of Arts in Philosophy, a Licentiate in Speech Communications from Trinity College, London, and is currently a Fellow candidate (FTCL).

Vicki is the Owner and Director of Outspoken Communications, a public speaking consulting company.

She is the fortunate recipient of numerous national and international awards for her writing.

www.outspokencommunications.com
www.linkedin.com/in/vickigoodfellowduke
www.facebook.com/Outspoken-Communications-
The-Public-Speaking-Experts-582956405194903

We Don't Know What We Don't Know

By Carole Kuypers

I may not know what I don't know but what I do know is that Carole works in an industry dominated by Masculine Energy and can do so standing strong and tall in her Feminine Energy. She is a perfect example of what we all need to strive for. Not all good financial decisions are reached solely from our minds.

MOST PEOPLE SPEND more time planning for a vacation than planning for the possibility of an illness, death or their own retirement. Why is that? Are they living day to day hoping for the best, or do they simply not realize there is a way to plan and protect themselves and their families?

Six years ago, my dear friend Julia was diagnosed with stage four cancer. Although she fought it heroically, it took her life in two short years. During those two years, I spent endless hours with her and her family. Between the numerous surgeries, radiation, and chemotherapy treatments, the hours were long but the days were short. Julia's children were six and nine at the time — the same age as my children. I helped out by driving them to and from school, often finding myself watching cooking shows with Julia after bringing the kids home. Her husband, Daniel, was under tremendous pressure as he continued to work full-time in order to support his family. He was run ragged trying to take over cooking, cleaning, and caring for his children and wife, assuming the additional roles of mother, father, husband, and Superman! Their daughter Mya was in a number of dance classes and their son Jacob loved to play soccer. Julia and Daniel felt it was important to maintain the extracurricular activities in order to allow the kids *to be kids.* Throughout the trauma, they all kept a positive attitude and were able to enjoy the indeterminate number of days Julia had left. I will never forget her big laugh and how she loved to joke around... it still warms my heart when I think of her.

Over time, their financial resources became strained and started to dwindle. There were additional costs associated with Julia's illness, and pressure to keep a sense of normalcy for the children. Both parents struggled knowing that Daniel would soon become a single parent supporting a family with only one income. The uncertainty of knowing how he was going to navigate this new life that was being forced upon him, without his soul mate, was devastating.

Julia's illness and eventual passing occurred prior to me becoming a planner with Investors Group. Although I knew the family well, I was not fully aware of their financial situation. As it turned out, Julia had just started a new career and was not yet eligible for the group life insurance coverage, something she had always counted on from her previous employers. It was only upon her passing that I learnt she was not adequately covered. I assumed their family had personal life insurance as I did, and naively believed that everyone purchases life insurance. Watching their family navigate life without life insurance opened my eyes to the necessity and the importance of knowing "what you have" in terms of family protection and a solid financial plan. Julia's situation made me take a closer look at my own coverage, and I realized that my own life insurance would leave my family grossly unprotected. Fortunately, I was healthy enough to put proper coverage in place shortly thereafter.

It broke my heart to lose Julia and watching her family struggle through the battle was equally heartbreaking. We are all notorious for wishing new knowledge on past situations, and the old cliché of feeling like "we wish we knew then what we know now" is hauntingly true.

No amount of money will bring Julia back, but a true financial understanding and proper planning could have made the family's situation less financially stressful. Daniel may have chosen to take more time off work to spend with his family, potentially hiring a caregiver for Julia, and getting some additional care for their young children. I often wonder how Julia felt watching her husband head off to work each day. Would she have preferred to have him by her side every day? Would she have preferred to see him have someplace to go that gave him a purpose and a reprieve from the raw emotion of watching his soul mate slip away little by little, day by day? My guess is that being the strong and opinionated lady she was, they would have driven each other a bit crazy had he been home every day. The most substantial impact that coverage for Julia would have made would have been eliminating the constant financial pressure Daniel felt. Losing the love of your life is hard enough without having to add financial hardship to the mix.

It is only natural to shy away from uncomfortable conversations and fearful situations. We often put things off until it is too late. No one gets married and plans for their spouse to have an untimely death. Nonetheless, death is a reality of life. You can't have one without the other. Many times life insurance coverage is only placed on the husband's life, as he is often the breadwinner of the family. It is common for couples to insure the husband, yet leave the wife unprotected. Couples often believe that when the wife takes on a stronger caregiver role, her financial value lacks the same significance as her husband's. If there is one thing that Julia's family taught me, it is that this belief is untrue. If something happens to the wife, everyone suffers. Not only is her potential income gone forever, there are several responsibilities that mothers typically manage, such as: shopping, cooking, cleaning, laundry, driving children to and from activities, and caregiving. These additional responsibilities can become very expensive for the widower.

Since taking on my role at Investors Group, I have come to realized how fast life can change at the drop of a hat. The impact of an illness, job loss, divorce or death can be devistating emotionally and financially. As women, we need to have a clear understanding of our own financial situation. Wills, life insurance and money are difficult topics to discuss openly, so they are often pushed aside to discuss at a later date.

If not now, when?

We will never be younger or healthier than we are today, so why wait?

We must let go of any discomfort and embrace the concept that *knowledge is power*. We can control our destiny to a certain extent by the decisions we make *today*. As a mother, I want to know that if I have an untimely death, my family would not be left in financial ruins. It is important to me that my children would continue to have the same opportunities and lifestyle with or without me. I take great comfort in knowing that my children will be able to attend a post secondary institution, enabling them to build a solid foundation for their own life's journey. No mother would choose to leave her precious family, but if that should happen, I want to know that she is satisfied she did all she could to protect her loved ones for years to come.

ABOUT CAROLE KUYPERS

Carole enjoys spending time with family and friends. She also enjoys reading, baking and loves to travel and experience other cultures. In her younger years, she spent 23 years as an owner operator of a number of retail stores across Alberta. As a consultant with Investors Group Financial Services, Carole enjoys guiding her clients in attaining their financial goals. Carole is passionate about empowering her clients through empathy, education and understanding.

www.carolekuypers.com
www.linkedin.com/in/carole-kuypers-0ab71b21
www.facebook.com/CaroleKuypersInvestorsGroup

Imperfection Is Not Your Reflection

By Heather Colberg

Heather shared her story publicly for the first time at Women Talk. I could feel her deep love and painful memories as she shared with the audience, who were shocked when her stunningly beautiful daughter Madison walked to the mic to share her gratitude. No one knew she was there. It was a powerful evening I will never forget.

How do you react when things do not go as expected? When things are not perfect?

On December 24th, 1995 I gave birth to my third child, Madison. Our family doctor, Dr. Lyle said, "Congratulations Heather and Kelly, you had a baby girl, however we have a couple of complications, so we will get you cleaned up and discuss a few things." My heart sank. I was disappointed I did not get to hold her. Then I got scared. My thoughts were racing about what could be wrong. Here is where my story *really* begins.

Kelly was holding me telling me everything was going to be fine. Thirty minutes after she was born, I finally got to see my bundle of joy for the first time. I took one look at those beautiful blue eyes and fell in love. Then I noticed something peculiar about her nose and lip. I never knew what a cleft lip and palate were. You see, Madison had a gaping hole in the roof of her mouth and her lip was attached to her nose.

The journey into my new life began.

Even though she had this defect, she was still the most beautiful bundle of joy in the world. Her crooked smile only made me fall in love with her more. I realized very quickly that breast-feeding would not be an option. Dr. Paulsen helped us invent a new way to feed Madison. The doctor took a bottle, wrapped a stick, and we tilted Madison almost upside down and squirted the formula into her mouth. We quickly realized if we didn't have her tilted the right way the milk would go right through the top of her mouth and out her nose, the poor thing.

The next day we received a special bottle from the Alberta Children's Hospital and it made feeding her much easier. We spent a few more days in the hospital adjusting to our new life.

Dr. Lyle came to visit daily and one day he said the most special words to me that I will never forget. He said, "I just wanted you to know that Madison is so lucky that she was born into your family. You, Kelly, and the boys will give her all the love and support she needs to get through this."

At that moment, I was not really sure what he meant. However, as time went on, his words would become evident.

Our first trip to the Alberta Children's Hospital was about a week after Madison was born. This was my first time visiting that hospital and I was amazed and overwhelmed by the number of sick children I saw. I soon learned that Madison's issues were small compared to many, which profoundly brought things into a humbling perspective along our journey.

We met Margaret from the Cleft Palate Clinic, who assisted us. She retired when Madison was 15 years old. This Cleft Palate Clinic was amazing! They explained all the processes we would have to go through with Madison, including: speech therapy, hearing tests, heart tests, breathing, dentistry, and surgery. My first job was to get her weight up to ten pounds. Now this seems like a small feat, however, you have to remember that the roof of her mouth was not closed and she was unable to nurse so it was hard to get weight on her. With determination, we accomplished our first mission in three months, and she was able to have her first surgery in February, 1996 to repair her lip and nose.

One year later, she had her second surgery to repair her palate. She was very excited as she could now eat solid foods. Madison was growing and developing like any other young child, although we knew she had more surgeries ahead.

At the tender age of six, she had bone removed from her hip for a bone graft to rebuild her gum line as it wasn't developing. This was probably the hardest surgery for all of us because she was old enough to understand what was going on. Her mouth hurt as well as her hip so we had to keep her settled. That Christmas, Kelly and I spent countless hours cutting out hundreds of paper snowflakes, which she absolutely loved.

Madison spent almost ten years of her life in braces and she never complained. She always followed her dentist's instructions to the letter and it shows. Today, she has the most beautiful smile.

She has a saying:

"Imperfection is not your reflection."

The next big surgery came in August, 2013 when she had to have her jaw broken and her lower face rebuilt. The surgeons were concerned that if they didn't fix this it could cause her joint pain issues as an adult. This surgery changed something else in Madison. While her jaw was healing, and she was having difficulty eating, she decided to explore the world of bodybuilding.

While school was always her first priority, her second priority became bodybuilding and she dedicated every spare minute to being the best she could be. She competed and although she didn't win, she won for every day from then on, because she transformed her body to what she had always wanted. Although she doesn't compete anymore, to this day, she still works out and has made physical fitness part of her lifestyle.

Through the years, Madison has only allowed a handful of true friends into her life, and for them, I am so thankful. They have accepted her for who she is, how she looks and have never once made her feel she was different. They know who they are and will always have a special place in her heart.

Madison began having difficulty breathing, and then her nose started collapsing. We went to see her doctor and he advised she would have to have bone taken from her other hip and rebuild the bridge under her nose. He scheduled her next surgery for April, 2014. The timing was horrible as it was one month before her high school graduation.

Madison declared, "Mom I can do this, I know it will get fixed and we will work hard to keep the swelling down. I will be ready to go to Grad." Well, true to her word, the big day came, and she looked absolutely stunning.

Madison went on to university to pursue studies in business. While in school, she received an email from Patti Falconer's modeling agency and was asked to come in for an interview. She was interviewed to compete in the Miss Universe Canada pageant. Several weeks passed by and she didn't hear anything. Then one day out of the blue, she received a telephone call informing her that she was selected as one of 52 contestants to compete in Toronto in May, 2015.

Madison was doubly ecstatic! Firstly, the pageant became a life changing experience, and secondly, the charity the pageant supported was Operation Smile. Operation Smile helps fund surgeries for children born with cleft lips and palates.

Madison placed in the top 20 and was recognized in three categories. She was also selected as one of the humanitarians to go to Nicaragua to see the actual surgeries at Operation Smile, visit orphanages and spend time with the children. She was able to watch first-hand what she had went through, right in the operating room. She observed the parents and came to realize what her dad and I had gone through with her. What an experience!

Today, Madison is dedicated to making a difference. She volunteers on numerous committees, loves to learn, and hopes to pursue law one day.

If you were to meet Madison today, you would think how lucky she is to be smart, beautiful and so kind. However, you would not know the trials and tribulations she has been through to get here. She is loved by so many and she gives so much love back to us all.

Watching Madison grow up these past 21 years has taught me that no matter what obstacles life throws at you, you must make the most of what you have. I can't wait to see what she does with the next 21 years!

Dr. Lyle once said she was blessed to have us, but I think it's the opposite ... we were blessed to have her!

I am reminded of one of Madison's favorite sayings:

"Let your smile change the world and remember,
Happiness is right under your nose."

This story is dedicated to the Alberta Children's Hospital, Cleft Palate Clinic, Dr. M. Bindman, Dr. T. Lim, Dr. D. Vincelli, Dr. R. Frank, Dr. D. McPhalen, Dr. M. Vacy-Lyle, Dr. D. Paulsen and Dr. A. Narvey for everything you have done for Madison and our family. Words could never explain the gratitude we have in our hearts.

ABOUT HEATHER COLBERG

Heather Colberg is happily married to Kelly for 32 years and has three beautiful children: Trent, Taylor and Madison. She spent 35 years growing the family business, *Hi-Way 9 Express Ltd*, and sold the company in 2011.

In 2013, Heather started *Made in the Shade Blinds & More* in South Central Alberta. After a successful and rewarding business experience, she sold the company in 2017.

Her newest venture is HCMLifestyle.com —*"Inspiring YOU to be the Best Version of Yourself"*. The website will share information on Inspiring Stories, Fashion, Business, Health & Fitness, Random Acts of Kindness, Book Reviews, Recipes, Travel, and much more. What is most exciting is that the content will be from everyday people with real stories.

Madison (daughter), Heather

www.hcmlifestyle.com
www.facebook.com/hcmlifestyle
www.instagram.com/hcmlifestyle

Just One Ride

By Hazel-Jane Kalyn

Hazel-Jane has lived a fascinating life. It hasn't always been easy for her but it has made her a caring, loving, wise woman. Listening to her share her stories always inspires me. Hazel-Jane is a strong leader who after years of living in her masculine energy decided to embrace her feminine powers. The world is a much better place because of it.

$\mathcal{M}$AGGIE, MY MOTHER, would always say, "Life is hard, but once you understand this principle then it no longer seems as hard!"

For 51 years, from the time I was seven years old, my Mom was very sick. There were continuous hospital visits, hundreds of medical specialists, countless operations and psychiatric assessments, every synthetic drug known to man, and still no answers. You face many hard days, weeks, months and years when someone you love has a chronic illness. There are also an abundance of life lessons that are strewn in your path to help you grow, learn, and develop as a person.

Have you ever had a life-defining moment? One of those moments where it becomes clear to you that, whatever the circumstances you are dealing with in life, that moment will be forever intertwined with your existence, despite any innocence, reservations, or objections you might have?

It was mid-morning on a cold, crisp winter day. I sat in the sun, on the floor beside my mom's rocking chair. My tiny body, wrapped in a lemon yellow, fuzzy nightie, quietly watched her. She rocked back and forth gently, hooking rugs, and staring blankly into space. She rarely spoke. She rarely interacted. She looked much older than her 35 years.

I thought, *what have they done to my beautiful, vibrant mother?*

It was so painful to look into my mother's once loving brown eyes and realize that the person I knew and loved was not really there.

It was, however, my 11th year which was the most difficult of them all. This was the year I realized I would need to embrace death in order to truly live life to the fullest, unencumbered by doubts and fears. This was the year I awakened to the reality that life is finite and we only have one life to live — *just one ride!*

A couple of months after my 11th birthday my grandmother, Jessie Hazel Bailey Broder, who, next to my mom, I loved most in the world, lost her four-year battle with cancer at the age of 65. It was a long, hard, ugly battle she fought! Her death, for me, was a bittersweet moment. I was glad to finally see her out of pain but I would forever miss the feeling of her beautiful, voluptuous hug. This was my first funeral.

Unfortunately, in that era, adults did not realize children felt the separation and pain of death as acutely as they did. I had loved my grandmother so much but the last time I saw her, her tongue was hanging out of her mouth due to a stroke, her skin had turned purple from countless needles, and every bone in her body poked through her transparent skin. I had a hard time giving her a hug. I could smell cancer and death everywhere.

I felt... afraid! I became overwhelmed with new feelings of loneliness and emptiness that I had never experienced before.

When I returned to school after my grandmother's funeral, we were told by our vice principal that we would have a substitute teacher for the next couple of months as our regular teacher wasn't feeling well. He was a young man in his late 20's or early 30's and he and his wife had just had a baby. He was a tough taskmaster but extremely caring, involved, and fair. He taught me one of my greatest lessons in life, "always accept responsibility for your own actions." Three months later, we were told he had died due to complications from Leukemia. I attended another funeral.

I questioned, *"How can this be? Why is this happening? Who do I talk to?"*

After the news of my teacher's passing, I went home, crawled into bed, and cried my heart out.

A month after my teacher died, one of our classmates, a young man by the name of Gary, just disappeared. He was a likable, extroverted, twelve-year-old! Everyone looked for him — his family, the police, our group of friends — but with no success. I felt a great deal of stress, as did all his friends, when we had no idea what had happened to him. Someone we hung around with every day was suddenly missing. Months passed, winter faded into spring, and they finally found his body in the woods. The authorities surmised he had wandered away from a friend's cabin, gotten lost and died of exposure. Another funeral!

I realized... no one is exempt from death... not even a twelve-year-old.

The pain of death just kept injecting itself into my life and there was nothing I could do about it. Death was in control of everything — it came when it wanted, took who it wanted, and dictated how it was going to happen. Death was powerful. It manifested the most powerful emotions I had felt and continue to feel to this very day. What do I do with these emotions? How could I harness them and make sense of the pain and disconnection I was feeling?

I desperately searched for answers and comfort.

My parents were avid readers and we had a room in our home filled with wonderful books and two comfy chairs. When my mom and grandmother first got sick, this room provided me with hours of solace when life seemed unbearable. I have fond memories of winter, when I would wrap up in a cozy blanket, drink hot chocolate, and read a wonderful book. This room was a treasure trove of interesting, adventurous, inspirational books: *The Power of Positive Thinking* by Norman Vincent Peal, *No One Hears but Him* by Taylor Caldwell, *Catch 22* by Joseph Heller, *The Grapes of Wrath* by John Steinbeck. I started to read everything I could about life and death.

I read!

And... I read!

And... I read!

The Tibetan Book of Living and Dying, The Power of Now, The Art of Happiness, Zen and the Art of Motorcycle Maintenance, Women Who Run with the Wolves, The Alchemist, all incredible, wonderful, brilliant books written by sensitive, diverse, talented authors from around the world.

Each book filled another piece of the puzzle, until the picture started to become clear... ***Life is not about the beginning or the end,***

but rather, it is about the journey in the middle. If you spend all of your time worrying about what the future will hold, you will miss the journey. Roads not taken because you were afraid you might not succeed, love not acted upon because of fear of rejection, adventures not taken because of concern for safety, and a life time not fulfilled because of a fear of death.

I mused... *is this what I wanted*? To look back in 40, 50, 60 years and say, "I wish I would have."

I now understood, at the tender age of 12, there is no life without death. Death was not the end but rather a whole new beginning. This was the year I learned a life-altering lesson, "I only get one opportunity to live this life as Hazel-Jane and I had better make the most of it... *you have just one ride!*"

It took me many more years of reading, discussing, and studying to fully understand and accept, to the point of total freedom, the inevitability of my demise. We are born to die, we just do not know when or how and nor should we. However, we must be aware that death is inevitable, so get out there and participate in life because who knows how long we each might have? Within reason, do what makes you happy.

Today, I love spending time with my beautiful children and grandson, visiting with dear friends, and having fun at the beach with my three furry family members. I also enjoy being a personal trainer with many fabulous clients, cooking and eating nutritious, delicious cuisine and sharing it with all who will come.

I'm an avid reader, gardener, skier, and swimmer. Adventuresome at times, I enjoy scuba diving, skydiving, jungle adventures, river boat adventures, and paramotoring to name just a few activities.

Forty-eight years after my first life-defining moment, I now understand there is a very fine line between the earthly plane and the heavenly plane. I can still hear my grandmother's voice, her laughter, and smell her skin. I can still feel the whiskers on the side of my grandfather's face and the pungent aroma of snuff as I reached up to hug him. I still remember, as if it were yesterday, misbehaving in church and the lecture I received from my teacher about accepting responsibility for my actions and the consequences for not doing so. I still remember my young classmate, who never had a chance, as I did, to see what life could have brought him and been given the opportunity to be grateful for it.

I learned... *ask not what is to come, but savour what is, and enjoy the ride we call Life.*

ABOUT HAZEL-JANE KALYN

Hazel-Jane Kalyn is part owner and personal trainer for Integral Training Services (It's Fitness), a company dedicated to total health and lifestyle wellness.

She earned her ACE Personal Training Certificate, American Council on Exercise, from the Elevated Learning Academy in 2012. Hazel-Jane continues to increase her knowledge and expertise by attaining fitness and nutrition certification accreditations. She is also a Fitness Nutrition Specialist and currently studying Weight Management Specialist Certification.

After many years spent practicing Interior Design, Ms. Kalyn decided it was time for a change and now dedicates her time and passion to designing bodies and lifestyles.

Her interests in fitness and nutrition have been a driving force in her life. She grew up in a sports-minded family who encouraged participation in many different sports: swimming, golfing, squash, baseball, basketball, skating, mountain hiking, anything for fun and activity. Combining exercise and proper nutrition has provided her with a healthy, active lifestyle.

Her greatest belief is *"health and wellness are the keys to happiness and success"!*

www.itsfitness.ca
www.facebook.com/integraltrainingservices
www.instagram.com/its_fitness_

Saved by an Angel Again and Again

BY DAWN JAMES

Have you ever met someone that intrigues you? A person that when you look at them you can't help feeling they know something that you don't. Dawn is such a person. She is connected to a "je ne sais quoi." Maybe her angels find her easy to talk to and that's why she has divine evidence to share in her shocking angelic story.

Brigitte

"Angels keep me safe"
— ANONYMOUS

WE DON'T NEED to see them or even hear them to know they exist. Sometimes their presence is felt with a 'hunch,' a 'gut feeling,' a scent, a melody. Sometimes they manifest as butterflies, birds or feathers. One thing I have come to realize is the important role angels have played in my life. Here are just two of the many instances where angels saved my life.

I will never forget the summer of 1978 as long as I live. It was my first recollection of what I like to call 'divine intervention.' My parents had a weekly ritual of going grocery shopping every Saturday evening. On this particular Saturday, I was dressed and anxiously waiting to go out — sitting on the stairs between the first floor and upper floor of our two-story townhouse. My Dad came down the stairs and passed me to put on his shoes, then opened the door and went to start the car. My mother followed next, and when she got to the front door and touched the door knob, I stood up and suddenly realized my feet could not move.

She turned to watch me on the stairs and asked, "Are you coming down?" There I stood, frozen in time, my feet glued to the stairs. I felt my lower jaw move and the words flowed out gently, **"I don't want to go."** As soon as I heard those words coming out of my mouth, my first thought was, *"what did I just say?!!"*

Mom then asked me, "Are you sure?" I felt increasing pressure pushing down on my shoulders. My knees finally bent to the downward pressure and I found myself sitting once more. I repeated the same phrase in a monotone voice, **"I don't want to go."** She accepted my answer and left with Dad on their 30-minute drive to the store.

When the sound of Dad's car motor finally faded from my ears, I felt the pressure on my shoulders lift away. I stood up and walked down the stairs. Most Saturdays we would finish grocery shopping within an hour. But I would soon come to realize that this was no ordinary Saturday. It had been three hours since my parents left without me. To calm my nerves, I began pacing up and down the kitchen where I could peer through the window to our parking spot in front our townhouse.

Three and a half hours went by. Then came a knock at the door, "Who is it?" I asked. "It's officer so and so, is this Dawn? Your parents are hurt and you will need to come with me." I was home alone, possessed a vivid imagination, and had watched more than my fair share of police shows. I asked the officer to walk over to the kitchen window and show me his badge, which he willingly presented. I asked him to wait outside while I called my godparents to tell them what had happened and that a police officer was waiting to take me to the hospital to see Mom and Dad. Luckily, my godparents lived nearby.

Within 15 minutes of the call, my godparents and I were sitting in the back of the police cruiser to go to meet my parents. I can still remember my godmother's warm hands holding my hands as I sat nervously in the police car on our way to the hospital. I sat with her in disbelief when I heard the police explain that my parents were driving home, when another vehicle in the opposite lane lost control and was heading towards them. To avoid a head-on collision, my dad swerved away from the oncoming car, but ending up hurtling across two lanes and his car flipped over into the culvert. Mom and Dad were both hurt and rushed to the hospital.

As my awareness returned to the present moment, I looked around the back of the police cruiser and that's when it hit me — the earlier incident on the stairs, my inability to move my feet, the pressure on my shoulders forcing me to sit down, and the unfamiliar voice telling my mother, "I don't want to go." What if I had gotten into the car with them? Would I have survived the car accident? Would I be alive today?

Although I felt lucky to be alive, I was never able to explain to my parents what had happened to me while I was on the stairs that night. I think I kept silent because of survivor guilt. I was okay but they had been hurt. I did not have the vocabulary to explain what had happened, nor did I have any concept of angels — not in 1978.

> *God not only sends special angels into our lives,*
> *but sometimes He even sends them back again*
> *if we forget to take notes the first time!*
> — EILEEN ELIAS FREEMAN

Flash forward 30 years

Have you ever noticed that life sometimes puts us in a loop and we relive the same patterns again and again? The first time I got into a car accident I forgot to take notes on what time the accident took place. However, six months later my eyes would be opened to a life pattern that was unfolding and the 'divine intervention' that I was not paying attention to. The second car accident I experienced occurred exactly six months to the day after the first car accident, at exactly the same time — 7:20 AM. To add more synchronicity to the event, my car was damaged in the exact same front area as the first accident, both accidents were hit and runs, and caused by male drivers.

Now they say that the third time is a charm.

I was driving my son to work one morning. His shift started at 7:30 AM so I typically dropped him off at work around 7:15 AM. On this particular morning, I dropped him off at 7:15 AM and headed down the main street to get to the highway on-ramp. About a minute into my drive I heard a strong male voice say to me, **"Pull over for ten minutes."**

My radio was off and I was alone in my car. What would you do if you heard that? I glanced over to the clock on the dashboard and it read 7:16 am. *"You have got to be kidding me,"* I thought. Then I remembered the date — today was exactly six months to the day since my second car accident and I was four minutes away from repeating an unhealthy life pattern.

"Trust the voice," I said to myself. I pulled over to the shoulder of the road, and I sat quietly, patiently and obediently for ten minutes. When the clock said 7:26 AM I turned on the ignition and headed towards the highway.

I had barely driven three kilometers when I realized why the angel had told me to, **"Pull over for ten minutes."** Ahead of me, was a collision involving a little silver car (the same make and color as my car) with the front end partially crushed behind an 18-wheeler long haul truck. The accident had happened recently because no police car or ambulance had yet arrived on the scene.

But the image I will never forget as long as I live is the face of the driver as our eyes met. He gently smiled as he saw my face and our eyes locked — he looked relieved to see me! **What???** The expression on his face told me, *"I am glad you are okay."*

Was he real? Was I dreaming? Was he an angel? I looked ahead when I heard the ambulance siren approaching the accident scene. When I arrived home, I remained in my car, in silence, for what seemed like an eternity. I tried to make logical sense of it all: the message, the time I received the message, pulling over for ten minutes, the accident on the highway, the man's facial expression — smiling at me. I am relieved that the six-month incremental pattern of car accidents was now broken.

Was he an angel? I don't really know. But one thing I know for sure... when angels speak to me... *I listen.*

I have received several angel messages over the past 40 years that have literally saved my life.

Sometimes the angel message comes through my intuition, sometimes through my dreams, and more recently, I can hear them speak. If you have encountered any of the signs I mentioned earlier, know that they are divinely placed to get your attention.

I truly believe that angels are messengers who are here to protect us and keep us safe. I am grateful to be *alive* and *living* and I am eternally grateful for the divine messages I receive.

ABOUT DAWN JAMES

Dawn James is the founder of raiseyour-vibration.ca, an organization dedicated to providing education, inspiration and support related to understanding and enhancing vibrational frequency for overall health and well-being. She is the author of the best-selling book *Raise Your Vibration, Transform Your Life: A Practical Guide for Attaining Better Health, Vitality and Inner Peace* (English and Spanish), and the book *How to Raise the Vibration Around You*. Dawn enjoys public speaking, teaching, and hosting retreats across North America, the UK, Mexico, Costa Rica, and beyond. Her second passion is assisting others to share their story through her publishing education company Lotus Moon Press.

Her soul's work is expressed at www.raiseyourvibration.ca
Her heart's work is expressed at www.publishandpromote.ca
www.facebook.com/raiseyourvibr8n

How to Plan for Your Extraordinary Life

BY PAULA COOK

Fun, witty, powerful are just a few words that can be used to describe this firecracker. Paula's dedication is one of the things I admire most about her. Whether she decides to travel, to be a great single mom, or to help women with their finances, Paula always instills her complete devotion. Every time this lady steps up to a mic, you know she is ready to deliver greatness.

THE EVENT THAT altered the course of my life was found in a Fortune cookie. *'Travel will change the course of your life.'*

I was 22 and living in Edmonton and I was determined that somehow, I was going to have an extraordinary life. A friend and I had just decided that we were going to pack up, like so many before us, and go over to Europe to find... something! Ourselves? Adventure? Love? The plan was to head over for six months but we bought one year, open-end tickets regardless. I came home two years later after having spent most of that time in Greece, specifically on the southern coast of Crete, attending to that 'love' aspect of my youthful adventures.

When I came back, I stayed in Calgary for roughly a year, but I just knew that I needed to find a way to work and live in Europe. That time, the plan was to stay for two to three years but 20 years later, and with my two adorable sons and Dutch partner that I was sponsoring, I finally returned.

I had spent all those years as a European Tour Guide and had lived in London most of the time, where I'd bought a small garden flat in West London. I also spent three years in Amsterdam, bought a house in

New Zealand in which to spend the off-season, and lived in Paris and Rome for extended periods of time.

I worked primarily in Western Europe but I did spend time in Russia, Scandinavia, and Eastern Europe as well as doing regional tours throughout Italy, France, Switzerland, Austria and the Benelux countries which are Belgium, The Netherlands and Luxembourg. I guided guests from Canada, United States, Australia, New Zealand, South Africa, Zimbabwe, Israel, India, Malaysia, and Pakistan to name a few, and I learned a lot of things about people. Americans are not the loudest nationality. The Scottish are not the ones with the shortest arms and deepest pockets. 'Fanny Pack' has many interpretations as does the name, "Randy" and one should never assume that your favourite sport of football is the same game worldwide.

I had it all! An enviable lifestyle, friends from all over the world, a lover here and there, disposable income, and the ability to travel all over the globe — which I took full advantage of — and most importantly, I'd achieved it all on my own. That, even at a young age, was tremendously important to me.

It's a funny thing thinking that you've got it all. You start to realize that what you chased as a younger person no longer has as much value as you get older. And the things that my teen sons think will never be a priority to them are what I found myself lacking: a sense of community, a sense of belonging, and an ability to give of myself to causes that are profoundly important to me.

I grew up in a family of women. My father was there, he provided us with the necessities, but I don't remember him ever making me feel loved, special, or adored and that leaves a huge impact on a young woman. My mother on the other hand, always was, and at the age of 84, still is our champion. So, I guess from an early age I've had the interests of women and children as my priority, because it was always 'us girls' and the lens that I looked at life through, that was influenced primarily by women.

When I came back to Canada in 2005, I tried to commute back and forth to Europe, but leaving my partner and kids behind was doing none of us any good. How and where was I to change careers at 44-years-old as one who'd never been in a traditional employee/employer situation and was not about to start? Oh, and I also needed to earn an income to support the lifestyle that I'd always provided for myself and fully intended to continue!

When a very close friend of mine, whose opinion I value highly, suggested that I go talk to Investors Group, I was open to the idea. I was someone who had bought and sold several houses, but had never needed to start an RRSP because I was never going to get old, had no idea what an NOA was, and had lost track of a $10,000 GIC that had been rolling over at 2% for years. I cringe at this very public admission but it shows how capable we all are, not just me. The huge advantage that I had at that stage of my life was that I was undefeatable! I'd taken chances all my life, won most of the time, had always earned a commission-based income, done well, and saw no problem continuing in that manner.

The vitally important thing that began to be apparent to me the more I continued my discussions with Investors Group, was that I was going to be able to check off almost all the boxes labelled, "What Is Important to Me." Freedom to work around my children was primary. The ability to work with the kind of people that I wanted to work with, another. The ability to grow my business at the rate and speed that I chose, within a company that would allow me to serve the women that I acquired as clients with the integrity, honesty and attention to detail that I set as my standard all my working life. From my first day with Investors Group nearly a decade ago, my focus has been to empower women financially.

The learning curve was enormous, but I worked hard, with dedication, and still went to every event that my children were involved in. Life back in Canada was great!! What could possibly go wrong?

Divorce.

I was told by people that divorce takes the wind out of your sails for three to five years. What they failed to mention is that for part of that period, you have no sails. You fall victim to the elements — burning heat, choppy seas, doldrums, hurricanes and lightning — and all you can do is bounce around and try not to be swamped and sink.

I became, and still am, a single mother. I'm pretty much solely responsible for the raising of my sons, both from a dedication and financial perspective. Let me shout it from the rooftops now, if it hadn't been for my family and friends and, in particular, my two sisters, I don't know what I would have done those first two years. The Sisterhood literally kept me from being swamped and losing my anchor, and I don't think that I'll ever be able to thank them or my friends enough.

The one thing that I was determined not to do was to become the cliché of the single mother, or should I say, what my idea of that was at the time. My own mother stayed in an unhappy marriage for a variety of reasons, one of them being that to be divorced was somehow shameful and had a very negative stigma attached to it. The other was that she was financially reliant on my father. She was educated and is intelligent but her generation bowed to the societal norms of, "the man works, the woman does everything else." Now, I'm proud to say that I'm a single mother because it's a hard job and anyone that has raised kids knows what a challenge it is, so doing it as a single parent makes me kind of bad ass!

Whenever someone comes to me right out of a divorce, I try to set them on the path of financial self-discovery. I've learned through the years that women far too often buy into the belief that 'someone or anyone' can do a better job of managing their money than they can, and the emotional battery of going through a divorce leaves them weakened and vulnerable. The one aspect of life that keeps us from going under during that time is the need to protect our children and not have them suffer.

Money means very different things to women that it does to men. Once a woman is financially secure, she is no longer solely motivated by money. She generally looks for an added spiritual component and how she can help others and improve the world. But to get there, she needs to take control of her financial situation and if it needs improving, then improve it! You want to explore the world? Get an advanced degree? Start your own company? Money is the foundation that all of it is built on, but people spend more time planning their annual vacation than they do attending to the financial foundation of their lives. You don't have to have unlimited supplies of money; few of us do, but you do have to be sensible and make it work for you. Make smart decisions. Perhaps it's time that women, like men, start using money to build up their ego, self-reliance and independence, and let go of feeling guilty about making money and providing a wonderful lifestyle for ourselves. When we do this, we can then plan for our extraordinary life. We've earned it!

ABOUT PAULA COOK

Paula Cook is one of the few born and bred Calgarians that you can find these days. She moved to Europe in her early 20's and lived primarily in West London and worked across the continent as a European Tour Director.

Both of her sons were born in Europe but eventually her desire to raise her boys close to her family, brought Paula back to Canada in 2006. She has always been passionate about helping women and children so when she joined Investors Group in 2008 she concentrated on empowering and educating professional women while developing trusting, long-term relationships.

Paula is a devoted parent to her teenage sons and enjoys watching them play soccer. She has taken up skiing again while her sons 'ride', she golfs in the summer, and is completing her CFP and Canadian Securities designations. She also enjoys cooking, red wine and lots and lots of laughter.

www.linkedin.com/in/paulacook
www.facebook.com/PaulaCook123

To Be or Not to Be
(A Nun)

By Suzn Morgan

Suzn made me realize early on just how important Women Talk is to women. She had an important message that she was burning to share and we were willing to listen and learn. This beautiful lady has a strong gift for compassion, and makes a difference in the lives of many.

WHAT ARE YOUR dreams? Do you follow them? Perhaps you do not know what they are because they are secret, so secret that you don't recognize them.

It took me years to discover that I had secrets, secrets I kept even from myself. I had an epiphany one day when a deeply buried and embarrassing secret suddenly surfaced. As I recall, I was ten years old when I first heard a whisper of a dream calling me. In that moment of inspiration I imagined that I wanted to be a nun! I remember my little body tingling and my heart racing wildly at the thought of becoming a nun.

As the years passed, my dream faded from memory. It was decades later when I rediscovered that truth, that secret... my secret aspiration to be a nun! And once I finally gave it a voice, I realized how that desire had become a constant longing in my life.

When I was that young girl, this is what "becoming a nun" meant to me:

It meant I could travel to faraway and unusual places.
It meant that I could help people.
And it meant that I didn't have to be married in order to do that!

Ah, how sweet and innocent was that dream that was seeking expression.

It was my authentic heartfelt aspiration. It was a profound yearning seeking expression. And funny enough, I was unaware that I might have to be religious to be a nun.

I was embarrassed to reveal that secret because, even decades later, I still felt so challenged and confused that I dare not reveal something so potent and authentically true about myself. I was always a shy, anxious, and naïve child. I was raised on a diet of no bragging, and no thinking you might be better than others. It was shame that made me subconsciously bury that ember of a calling deep inside. There were moments in my younger days when I sensed that inner ember. It stirred in me like multi-coloured leaves swirling lightly in the wind on a crisp fall day.

In grade seven, I heard about someone from my small hometown who had recently moved to a faraway place called "Belize." He went to live in the untamed jungle on a river. When I heard about his adventure, I felt a stirring in my belly. Years later, there was a big earthquake in Mexico City. I felt troubled for months by a deep urge to go there to help. Every night I dreamed about packing my suitcase and going, yet I never voiced that desire.

At 38 years of age, I finally followed my heart's longing. I went to Mexico to try to understand this mysterious yearning. I left my job, my family, and my community. I told them that I'd return in six months or six years! I would either just go have a look or maybe, just maybe, I would unearth the reason I felt so compelled to go there.

Going to Mexico was one of the bravest things I have ever done. I had never travelled anywhere before, and I did not speak one word of Spanish. The experience was scary, lonely, and the best adventure ever! Taking this leap into the abyss challenged the very fabric of who I knew myself to be. I realized there was more to me than my self-limiting beliefs and self-perceptions. I was challenged, expanded, and profoundly changed.

I remember the day I stood stock-still on a street in Mexico, just grinning like a fool. I could not believe my ears! Two people had just walked by chatting in Spanish, and I understood *one word* of what they said. One word! I felt such a burst of excitement recognizing just that *one word*.

I had enrolled in a course to learn Spanish, and althrough I learned the words I rarely spoke them. Why would I? If I ever said, "Buenos dias" (good morning) or the polite, "Como estas?" (how are you?), then people would respond in Spanish. I was never able to understand their reply. I would shrivel up with embarrassment. I just knew that I would never be able to decipher it. Then, on a sunny Mexican street, my world broke open. That was the day I understood *one* word in Spanish as though it had been spoken in English. I had finally arrived!

That experience shifted something inside me. I had a deep-seated belief that, "Only other people, smart people, could learn another language. Not ME!" And there it was, a significant and profound shift. I could learn and I did learn, a new language. By travelling to this new place, I had discovered a new aspect of myself. In doing so, I transformed that limiting belief. As I continued living in Mexico more experiences challenged old self-concepts. The dominoes began to fall and I grew and I flourished.

For the next six and a half years I lived and worked in both Mexico and Guatemala. I went from identifying myself as a stranger in a strange land to being deeply connected, concerned, and compassionate for the people I met — for their humanity and their suffering. I learned so much from the people and the culture. I was also fortunate to find work in Mexico at a social justice education centre and later with a child sponsorship project. I grew roots, deep roots, on this journey. I now realize I was manifesting that adventurous reverie from my childhood.

A grave breast cancer diagnosis caused me to return to live permanently in Canada. Nonetheless, I returned regularly to visit those dearly loved people and places. I continuously looked for ways to strengthen my connections and to be of service.

In 2013, during a trip back to Guatemala, I shared my journey with breast cancer with the women to whom I felt closest. As I shared my story, I discovered that there was a deep thirst among them for basic knowledge of breast cancer and its treatment. I was asked questions that I felt ill-equipped to answer. My own story was not enough. These women were left with many unanswered questions.

One woman came back to see me. Thirty-year-old Alicia, a vibrant single parent of three children, wept as she hesitantly peeled back a homemade dressing and showed me an appalling sore on her breast. She had been treating it for over a year with herbs and compresses but it wouldn't get better. I felt heartbroken as I told her it seemed serious and she needed to go see a doctor at the community health centre. She sorrowfully recounted how she had been saving a few dollars to go see the doctor but that one of the children had found her savings and taken it. Her future and that of her children were in jeopardy.

I was profoundly moved to return to Canada, research answers to the questions I had encountered, and return with valid information. That led me to create the *It's About Time! Cancer Awareness Project*. It garners support for basic breast health and breast cancer education for the most disadvantaged and underserved women and girls in Guatemala. My dream, my calling, had not been just to travel but to do something worthwhile in the world. I continue to be deeply committed to this compelling and necessary work. By encouraging and empowering women through education, I am manifesting my childhood dream of helping others.

Women have been a keystone in my life leading the way, and have mentored and nurtured me. Years ago, when I encountered feminist thought, I discovered an approach of critical thinking that helped me make sense out of so many confusing experiences. Perhaps most compelling was that I also learned that I can genuinely be vulnerable and strong, confused and visionary. This analysis helped me to overcome harsh self-judgment and to craft a much more connecting experience with others, especially women.

Through the years, the friendship, support, and leadership of other women has inspired, taught, and sustained me. From them I learned that we all need dreams. We need to find ways to connect to them. I believe that if we deeply want something we've never had, we have to do something we've never done. We have to be willing to take a chance. We can audaciously (and at times fearfully) and intentionally step forward into our future. Although we may feel alone, we're not. We are all women on the path, taking chances together.

As I continue to explore these magical, mysterious, and life-sustaining pathways, I have come to see that my youthful desire to "not be married" was the impetus that propelled me to make my own choices and discover my own authentic voice.

So, in the end, here I am:

Travelling to exotic places!

Helping people!

And not needing to be married to do so!

My childhood dreams came true!

ABOUT SUZN MORGAN

Suzn has been immersed in cross-cultural living and education for decades. She is the founder of the *It's About Time! Cancer Awareness Project* and *Gringo Lingo: Latin America Tours & Cross Cultural Training.*

With *Gringo Lingo* she employs her extensive expertise on the ground in Guatemala and Mexico to create enjoyable, impactful, and educational experiences. These are more than 'look & see' tours, rather they are designed to create connecting experiences.

The *It's About Time! Cancer Awareness Project* works in Guatemala with grass roots women's organizations to bring breast health and breast cancer education to rural women.

If you want to better understand the multicultural world around you, arrange for your group to be inspired by one of Suzn's engaging cross-cultural training workshops or presentations. *Suzn can help you create your own connecting experiences!*

www.itsabouttimeproject.com

www.gringolingo.ca

Wake Up and Take Your Leap!

BY SUSANNE HEATON

I think Susanne loves faeries because she is like a living, wise, magical, powerful faery herself. I like to call her my "pocket faery." When I need sage advice, I pull her out of my back pocket, she waves her wand, and the perfect, logical yet spiritual solution appears! Susanne will take you on her insightful journey from the corporate world to the world of nature's angels.

Brigitte

HAVE YOU EVER dreamt of doing something different in your life, but felt trapped by or scared of what others might think? After working in the fast-paced corporate world for over 11 years, I took a total leap of faith to start living some of my dreams after experiencing some life-changing wake-up calls. I've been known to be a little stubborn, so it took more than one wake-up call to make me take this leap.

The first wake-up call happened in 1998. I was diagnosed with Malignant Melanoma which is the most aggressive form of skin cancer. At the same time, I was finishing my second degree in Management and majoring in Marketing, and had previously accepted a corporate job that was to start when I graduated. The doctor told me that I had to schedule surgery, and although it wasn't an emergency, it was urgent and had to happen within the next two months. I went into an absolute tailspin, and I remember saying, *"What am I doing going into this corporate job? It is not what I really want to do."* I went for the surgery and thankfully, I only had Stage 1 Malignant Melanoma. Fortunately, it had not yet permeated the epidermis, so I didn't need any radiation or chemotherapy. After I was given a clean bill of health, I quickly fell into the old groove and I went into that corporate job.

The second wake-up call happened in 2002, when my friend's 12-year-old daughter, Sarah, was diagnosed with a rare brain tumour. She fought a very courageous battle, but sadly passed away in December 2003. The night after Sarah crossed over, she came to me in a dream. She was back to her giggly, mischievous old self and twirling in a meadow filled with wild flowers, she pointed to her shoulders and said, *"Susanne, I have faery wings instead of angel wings, because they are so much easier for running and playing around in the meadow."* When I woke up from that dream, I started to research everything I could about faeries. I found out that they are considered *"Nature's Angels"*, are a wee bit mischievous and want us to lighten up and play more in our lives.

I had done various things to raise funds in Sarah's memory, but I always knew in my heart that there was something more that I was meant to do. In March 2008, my husband and I were on a sea kayaking trip in Belize, surrounded by nature, when the entire inspiration for writing my book, *The ABC Field Guide to Faeries,* came streaming into my consciousness. I literally could not write the ideas down quick enough. I knew that Sarah and all of nature was helping me to tap into this creative channel. In the first ten days of that trip, I had the initial draft half completed. When I returned home, I decided that by May of 2008, I wanted to have the entire initial draft of the book completed. I achieved that goal.

Then in June 2008, I received my third wake-up call. I had been doing a fair bit of overseas travel for my corporate job and was putting in a lot of overtime. I was constantly exhausted and it took every ounce of strength to drag myself out of bed at 5:30 am, get to work, come home, eat, and then go right to bed. I was literally sleeping through my entire weekends. I was sure that I had caught a bug on one of my overseas flights. I went to my doctor, he ran some tests, and the results were that I was burnt out and needed to take a leave of absence from work, or end up in the hospital. That was a huge piece of humble pie for me to swallow as I had always been known to have so much energy and enthusiasm. It was hard to admit that I needed this downtime.

In November 2008, my fourth wake-up call occurred. My father, who had been struggling with chronic Leukemia, was getting worse and the doctors could not figure out why. The bottom line was that they had missed a six-inch cancerous tumour on his liver. When a tumour gets to that size, surgery, chemotherapy, or radiation are not an option. You are only told how much time you have left. Dad was given approximately three months and he passed away on January 20, 2009. I was lucky enough to be with him during his last months and keep him at home at our family farm in Manitoba. During one of our heart-to-heart talks, my dad looked at me and said, *"Sus, get yourself out of that corporate job, and go and focus on writing your book."* Because my father had been so proud of my accomplishments with my career, those words had a huge impact on me.

Upon returning to Calgary, I received a call from work asking me when I would return. My decision became very clear. I submitted my resignation effective March 15, 2009. An interesting thing happened immediately after that. Someone who I knew and respected that had worked for the company for over twenty years, confided in me that he wished that he had the same courage as me to leave. He said that he knew within the first two weeks that the company was not for him, but that he had gotten addicted to the money. His comments made me realize that I was not only going to write the book, but I would inspire people to live their life fully by following their heart's desires.

Has this leap of faith been a smooth ride? Absolutely not! Has it been worth it? Absolutely! The initial reviews for my manuscript were very positive and everything seemed to be falling serendipitously into place. I had an amazing illustrator that helped to make every faery come to life in the book. And then, it happened. I had a bestselling Canadian author agree to review my book. I was so excited that she had accepted, until I read her review. She said that my book was, *"Too Hallmarky, too romantic, not saying anything new, and not her cup of tea."* She also said that if I wanted to read really good poetry to read Dennis Lee's *Alligator Pie*. I was devastated. I was one month away from going to print. The inner critic in my head started to say, *"Who do you think you are, anyway? You are not an author."* After many tears and a good pity party, I decided to go to the library and check out Dennis Lee's poetry book as it had been a while since I had read it. When I read the first poem starting with the line, *"Alligator, Alligator, Alligator Pie,"* I burst out laughing. I realized that this bestselling Canadian author had no idea of what I was trying to say. She helped me to understand that not everyone was going to like my work. Not everyone has the same taste in music or movies or books, so not everyone would like or even understand what my book was about. There is a saying that goes, *"Sometimes those who hurt us the most are our biggest angels in disguise."* This reviewer ended up being that angel for me. As I researched a little more, I found out that numerous classic books were *"rejected"* when first approaching publishers: *Jonathon Livingston Seagull*, *The Diary of Anne Frank*, and *Harry Potter*, just to name a few!

The results of me taking this leap of faith continues to evolve as I travel down this road we call life. To date, I have received numerous awards including Best Book USA for Inspirational Poetry, sold over 5,000 copies of the book, raised over $20,000 for worthy causes, spoke to thousands with inspirational talks and workshops, and helped to keep Sarah's memory alive. All of this would not have happened if I had listened to that one reviewer's feedback.

I am passionate about sharing my story as well as techniques to inspire people to live their dreams and climb their own mountains in life. It fills me with joy when people share how my book or my talks have helped them through difficult times and given them the courage to pursue their dreams. *May you take that leap from your head to your heart and live the life you have always dreamed of. This world needs what you have to offer. Take that leap and let your light shine brightly.*

ABOUT SUSANNE HEATON

Susanne Heaton is one of the Directors for the Calgary Chapter of Women Talk. Her company, *Motivated by Nature*, offers tools to scale your own mountains in life through marketing consulting, mentoring, inspirational speaking, workshops, writing and creating mindful awareness. Susanne's skills have been acquired through formal training as well as personal reflection.

She has a Management and Marketing degree as well as a Physical Education and Recreation degree. She uses her own life to reflect on lessons learned as seen in her talk about climbing Mt. Kilimanjaro. She is a qualified Reiki Master, certified Heart Speak Level 1 practitioner, and Doreen Virtue certified Oracle Card reader.

She believes in lifelong learning and credits nature with being one of her greatest teachers. Susanne is motivated by nature. She looks forward to connecting with you.

www.motivatedbynature.com
www.facebook.com/Motivatedbynature1

Where My Psychic and Spiritual Experiences Have Taken Me

By Dr. Beth Hedva

If you ever get the chance to have tea with Dr. Hedva, make sure to take your smart pill beforehand. She is truly one of the smartest, most knowledgeable women I have ever met — even her teapot had me enthralled! Residing in her Divine Feminine Energy, she helps not only the people around her, but the entire world cope with trauma. It is truly an honour to know this fabulous, powerful woman.

QUESTION: HOW DOES a 12-year-old deal with psychic experiences like precognitive dreams and handle communicating with the dead (ghosts)?

Answer: She believes it is normal and acts polite by *not* talking about it.

That 12-year-old was me and I had no idea back then that helping others deal with *it* would become a profession.

The psychic abilities of my youth did not fully awaken into richer spiritual insights until I confronted what psychologists often refer to as a "crisis." The 1967 Detroit race riots turned my hometown into a war zone. Soldiers in tanks were called in just after the Merchandise Mart near my home was burnt to the ground. Five days of fires and looting left the downtown core decimated. Then in the spring of 1968, the assassinations of civil rights leader Martin Luther King and presidential candidate Bobby Kennedy filled the media. Social unrest and fear were everywhere. As family, friends, and neighbours fled the city, seeking safety in the suburbs, I was about to go through inner change.

First, I began to doubt whether God existed. At summer camp, I engaged in philosophical discussions about not "believing in God" with one of my camp counsellors. To inspire more thinking, he posed what might be one of the most clichéd of all philosophical questions: *"If a tree falls in the forest, and no one is there to hear it fall, does it make a sound?"* I decided, like God, that tree did not exist except within my mind's interpretation of it.

I became very good at making things not exist — God, trees, people, and soon, even I did not exist — other than in my own mind. But for me, as I was not yet 13, the world seemed crazy, so I decided, *"If I do not exist, then I am free! And if I am free, then I can do anything I want."* This was completely liberating!

I expressed my "freedom" by leaping in the air around the camp to see if I could lift off and fly like I do in my dreams. This did not sit well with one of my camp counsellors, who ridiculed me. I was shocked, hurt, angry, and confused! I felt misinterpreted and unable to "make him understand" how I was testing my new theory. Long story short, I could not make my feelings "not exist."

"Something exists — what is it?" I asked myself. I realized the only thing that could make me feel this way was my own mind.

Suddenly, I felt an awakening. I had a vision of each person, every tree, everything on earth, and everything in the universe, as small slices of a single giant pie. Instead of being isolated and *alone* — I realized we are *all one* — all tiny slivers of that one "pie." At 12 years old I experienced that universal mind as a mystical state of oneness. Because my slice of pie was made up from the same stuff as the rest of the pie, I gathered that we all could *know* and understand each other's thoughts and feelings. I *saw* and *felt* just how connected we all are. That shock and existential crisis, followed by genuine inner guidance, expanded me beyond my ego. My new-found inner guidance showed me how the universe speaks to us in symbols and I decided to learn that language.

After that day, my life seemed to be guided by a higher intelligence. When I returned from camp to our new home in the suburbs we went to visit my grandparents for Friday night dinner. After dinner, when everybody was visiting, I took the opportunity to browse my grandfather's library. I found a 1927 edition of Chiero's *Palmistry for All*. I also received a gift of tarot cards that summer.

My grandfather, Wolf Snyder, was a Yiddish scholar who studied the Kabbalah. The Kabbalah's teachings on the "Tree of Life" describe how we live in many worlds: a material, physical world as well as emotional, mental, spiritual worlds, and an energetic, limitless, divine world. The suits in the Tarot represent these worlds in pictures and symbols to show what life is like in each one.

My grandfather's palmistry book and the tarot cards were my introduction to how everything in our physical world could be a symbolic representation of much more. My interests grew for subjects like dreams, palmistry, numerology, astrology, talismans, gems, aromas, herbs, mysticism, and Eastern philosophies. I wanted to know how everything in our physical world reflects universal spiritual principles. By the time I turned 13 the separation between spirit and matter, between inner and outer worlds, disappeared.

Since then, my life has been spent weaving the psychic, psychological, and spiritual into the tapestry of daily life. When I began plans to attend college, my mother suggested I study with Dr. J. B. Rhine. He had coined the term ESP and founded an institute for the scientific study of extrasensory perception after retiring from Duke University.

I was the youngest member in the Institute's Summer Study Program when I joined at age 18. Besides experiments on ESP and psychic phenomena, phone calls (many of which I was to answer) flooded into the Institute daily from across America from people dealing with everything from ESP, reincarnation, and ghosts to UFOs. At that time in history, parapsychology was focused on statistically proving psychic phenomena existed. For those who *understood*, it was different. Personally, I thought we needed a "clinical parapsychology" that integrates the energetic, psychic, spiritual, and psychological dimensions into counselling. I saw my job as helping people identify and separate the psychic threads of experience from the psychological threads and spiritual threads.

After I finished my Bachelors degree, I travelled to California to visit parapsychologist John Palmer at JFK University. During my visit, I found out about JFK's new dual Masters: an MA in Clinical Psychology and MA in Transpersonal Counselling Psychology. I was in the right place at the right time and enrolled in the first accredited academic program in transpersonal psychology in the nation.

In my clinical work, I saw all kinds of people with all kinds of issues. Some, like Doris, came to me complaining about a ghost. "Why do you think the ghost came to you?" I asked Doris. "Could you need extra support for some reason?" We explored whether the ghost came to *give* or *gain* support. Doris agreed to a tarot reading, but seemed more interested in understanding the ghost than understanding herself.

Six months later, Doris returned. The ghost was no longer the issue. Her husband had, "a habit of drinking too much and he just walked out on the family." Then her five- year-old daughter, Sylvia, was brought before Child Protective Services for teaching her girlfriends sexually provocative games, which Sylvia apparently learned from her older cousin Dawn, who learned them from Doris's brother.

A shocked Doris finally opened up, committing herself to ensure her children would not suffer from neglect, physical, sexual and emotional abuse like she had, having had an abusive alcoholic father and mother who denied the abuse.

Doris realized she would consciously leave her body and view the abuse from "above." She'd also used other psychic gifts to "read" and avoid danger. In our sessions, she began using the same abilities she'd used to escape in a *new way* to perceive reality, accept "what is", and speak up and set clear limits with her family. Doris also learned to call upon her spiritual guides to help feel secure and be present for her daughter and family in new ways.

Doris' recently deceased friend John gave her inner strength, which allowed her to ask her husband to leave until he dealt with this drinking problem. In another incident, John identified tests Doris needed to correct a hormone imbalance which was causing her health problems.

Doris got tested and the imbalance was confirmed. The doctor was curious to know what specialist had referred Doris to him. Doris told him about John who had communicated to her "from the other side." Although chosen randomly from a list, this doctor "coincidentally" wrote papers on exactly the unusual imbalances the tests revealed. By being true to her inner guidance, Doris found healing and helped her doctor open his mind and grow too.

In 1989, I completed my Ph.D. dissertation, *A Community Model for the Uses of Intuition in Clinical Practice.* I described how crisis and trauma can take us through a psychic death that may awaken into a spiritual re-birth which can help us *and* others grow. Today, I call this a "trauma-induced spiritual awakening." I later tested the efficacy of my spiritually directed therapy under severe circumstances in Indonesia — the 2004 tsunami and loss of 170,000 people living under civil war conditions.

I never could have imagined nor planned for the doors that have opened from my ability to listen and follow my own inner guidance. I embraced my gifts, was willing to say "yes", and trusted the process. More than ever, I see how every experience in our lives becomes part of our spiritual journey of awakening. And if we allow it, we are guided to make our lives and the world we live in a better place.

ABOUT DR. BETH HEDVA

Author, teacher, and licensed psychologist, Dr. Beth Hedva blends conventional psychological practices with cross-cultural healing practices, including ancient and contemporary spiritual traditions. She trains professionals and lay audiences globally to use intuition and integrative therapies to tap new dimensions of inner healing. Dr. Hedva has been a Board Director of the International Council of Psychologists and is currently Director of Training and Counselling Services for the Canadian Institute for Transpersonal and Integrative Sciences.

Dr. Hedva held core faculty appointments in Antioch University's Department of Clinical Psychology, and JFK University's Department of Consciousness Studies in California. She has a Masters in Clinical Psychology, a Masters in Transpersonal Psychology and a PhD in Psychology. By invitation, she presented her trauma recovery techniques at the United Nations, was an "Expert Intuitive" for California's Office of Paranormal Investigation, and as a leading relationship expert was the On-Line "Ask an Expert" for Reader's Digest Canada.

www.drbethhedva.com

The Journey Home

BY BEV JANISCH

A few months after attending Bev's meditation class, my life plunged into personal turmoil. Bev's teachings were crucial in helping me to make it through and put my life back together. I believed Bev to be shy and quiet, until she shared her story at Women Talk. She ignited the room with an electrifying energy and had everyone dancing and celebrating their own stories.

Brigitte

> *"To thine own self be true."*
> — WILLIAM SHAKESPEARE

*H*OW CAN YOU be true to yourself when you don't know yourself? How can you feel deeply connected in your relationships without losing yourself and compromising your own needs and desires? Who are you when you let go of the roles that define you?

When I found myself asking these questions, I felt like I was the only woman who ever struggled to know myself, use my voice, and live in alignment with who I was meant to be. I felt alone and that everyone else had it all figured out and was happier and more content than I was.

So, I decided to start what I called "The Kitchen Table Series" and invited a group of women to come and sit around my kitchen table. We agreed to be vulnerable, share things that mattered, and open ourselves up to explore things that would make us feel uncomfortable. We made a pact that we were going to leave our "everything is fine" mask at the door. What we found was that below the surface, many of us were struggling with the same things and that we didn't always feel we had a safe place in which to be open, vulnerable, and honest. I will forever be grateful to these women who opened their hearts as we connected and explored what mattered most to us. In that process, we realized that we weren't alone.

What I came to learn from our kitchen table chats was that women have a lot in common even though it appears on the surface that we're all so different. Many of us struggle with using our voices in a way that aligns with the deepest truths about ourselves.

Perhaps the single biggest challenge in my own life was learning how to use my voice and live in alignment with my own needs and desires. My journey with this began with a memory that is etched in my mind forever.

When I was about seven years old, I was in Brownies and there were around 20 of us sitting around in a circle on the floor. I had to go to the bathroom so bad but was too afraid to put up my hand and ask permission to leave the circle. So, I peed on the floor and when I got up there was a big puddle. I felt so humiliated and ashamed and yet didn't feel I could share it with anyone.

Looking back, peeing on the floor that day in Brownies was a symptom of the fact that I couldn't make my needs known. I was too afraid to say what I needed and for whatever reason wanted to be small and invisible. My needs just didn't matter... I had lost my voice.

I took my inner girl silence and disconnect from my soul into my marriage, my relationships, my work, and basically my whole life. I was a little girl masquerading as an adult woman with a successful career, great husband, and countless things to feel grateful for.

As the years went by, I was so busy raising a family and working that I didn't take the time to get to know that little girl in me that couldn't use her voice. It wasn't until many years later when the universe created inner turmoil in me that I had to pay attention.

That inner turmoil that many of us experience is a wake-up call because it is your soul saying, "You have a deep yearning for certain things in your life and you're meant to pay attention to those yearnings. If you don't pay attention, this feeling of constriction and unrest will continue until you wake up and begin to listen to what I am trying to tell you. You are meant to heal your life, and in order to do that, you need to do some inner work. Are you going to rise to this challenge and make some changes or are you going to slowly wither away?"

In response to my soul speaking to me and with significant resistance, doubt, and skepticism, I began to study and practice meditation and mindfulness. I wasn't doing it to be spiritual, I was doing it because I knew the answers to what were missing in my life were inside of me and I really had no other idea how to tap into that part of myself and my inner voice. I used the tools to help me connect with what was important to me, what I valued, what made me come alive, what was holding me back, and for the first time in my life, to develop a relationship with the divine and get to know myself as a spiritual being.

As I sat for short periods of time in meditation, I realized that I had been using distractions and busyness as part of a subconscious conspiracy to avoid dealing with the stuff in my life that needed to be dealt with.

I hadn't lost my inner voice... I had been ignoring it.

As the days went by and turned into weeks and then months, I could feel myself healing. I was getting to know "Bev", both the little girl in me that needed to be loved, and the grown woman that was moving forward and living an empowered life. I could feel myself coming home to myself and healing from the inside out.

I began to see that the thing that is missing for many women is the awareness that you're meant to have needs, wants and desires and that if you compromise your core values in order to make things work, you'll end up feeling like something is missing in your life.

As a woman, you have an inner voice that is meant to be listened to and acted upon, and sometimes conflict is the result of using your voice. And while it's not comfortable, it's okay. Conflict and discomfort are often necessary for growth so that we can step fully into our best selves.

You need to know that your soul tries to connect with you through your inner yearning and longings that may feel like dissatisfaction and restlessness. Instead of ignoring these yearnings, it's important that you turn towards them and begin to understand what they are trying to tell you. They may be telling you that you need to make changes in your relationships, or that you need to engage in meaningful work, or that you need to step outside your comfort zone, or that you desire some alone time or have a craving for inner peacefulness, or need spiritual connection or more fun and adventure in your life.

As you begin to honor these yearnings and realize that they are part of a divine plan, the universe now asks that you take inspired action to live in alignment with your highest and best self. No more avoiding, blaming, complaining, hiding, playing small... it is time to bloom.

> *"And the day came when the risk to remain tight*
> *in a bud was greater than the risk it took to bloom."*
> —ANAIS NIN

The beautiful thing is that the soul knows what it needs to bloom and when you learn how to listen to that inner wisdom you will be gently guided towards knowing what needs to happen to grow from a bud to a full, vibrant, and stunning bloom.

Spending time getting to know yourself and listening to your inner voice is about living your life from the inside out. Hearing your voice enables you to remain grounded and aligned with your soul amidst an utterly chaotic world. It enables you to feel and honour all your emotions from sadness and loss to joy and contentment. You begin to take radical responsibility for your life. You make an agreement to be self-compassionate and to make friends with your inner critic. You care enough about yourself to carve out space for quiet in order to connect with the divine energy that flows through you and links you to your higher purpose. You become courageous enough to identify and own the beliefs that are holding you back and then pluck them out one by one and replace them with beliefs that are nourishing for your soul.

This journey inward is necessary in order to return to that place where inner peace is the springboard for living a deeply meaningful and empowered life. I have traveled to many exciting places including the top of Mount Kilimanjaro, and I can honestly say that the inner journey is the most exciting, exhilarating, adventurous, challenging, courageous, rewarding, inspiring, and life-affirming trip that you will ever take. And once you've taken your inner journey you will arrive home to a place where you know yourself, honour what you need, and move beyond the fear to use your voice to live in alignment with your highest self.

ABOUT BEV JANISCH

Bev Janisch is a coach, speaker, author, and founder of The Compassionate Mind. Bev mentors women who are ready to take an inner journey to connect with themselves, let go of what's holding them back, gain clarity about who they are and what's important to them. Bev believes that when women live life from the inside out, they experience greater meaning, fulfillment, and peace of mind.

Bev empowers women with a proven mindfulness-based system of powerful tools and techniques to transform their lives. Bev's 30 years as a nurse and her current expertise as a certified mindfulness and meditation teacher assist her in setting the stage for profound transformations. Women who work with Bev are guaranteed to ignite their inner sparkle. To learn more about Bev, meditation, or coaching visit:

www.thecompassionatemind.com
www.facebook.com/TheCompassionateMind

Stories That Stain and Stories That Serve

By Tammy Plunkett

Tammy is an accomplished writer and coach who helps many women to write their stories. Some people let adversity harden their soul but not this lady. She lives her life with an open heart and mind, the way we should all strive to. Grounded, spiritual, and caring, Tammy is a great addition to our tribe and a perfect example of the strong feminine energy.

My EVERYDAY LIFE is immersed in stories. I hear stories from life coaching clients and aspiring authors who share their deepest wounds and the powerful lessons learned from their challenges. Unfortunately, very few people escape childhood and early adulthood without some sort of trauma that alters the course of their life or sense of safety or identity on some level.

In the world of self-actualization and self-development, we put a lot of weight and importance on those earlier stories of struggle. They are the things we are meant to overcome on our hero's journey, they explain our wounds, and all too often they can also hold us back from the full freedom of happiness.

The battle between how much to share, how often, who to share it with, and the problem of identifying with and wearing our past stories was very clear to me during a retreat to Kripalu one autumn weekend a decade ago.

I drove up through the stunning fall colours of the Adirondacks to a retreat I had been planning for and longing to attend for months — a weekend full of yoga and workshops focused on journaling and developing a deeper relationship with myself. This was my idea of heaven on earth at a time in my life when I was a busy single mom trying to find myself again after my divorce.

Our workshop cohort consisted of people from everywhere and all walks of life. And, of course, we all had our own stories which we were asked to share with each other for a specific writing exercise. Or at least that was the intention of the workshop until Jennifer started to speak.

Jennifer was a round lady in her early forties who carried her whole body with the weight of the world resting on her back, on her eyelids, and on her tongue. She moved slowly and spoke slowly, and yet for all her lack of energy she consumed all the energy in the room. She relished attention and if she wasn't the center of it, she slowly but eventually commanded it.

Her story was an all too familiar one. She didn't get the love and attention she sought as a child, she'd been bullied in grade school, and learned to be invisible in high school for her mere survival. In university, she'd been dating a fellow she absolutely adored for about a month when he got drunk one night and forced himself on her and left her half-naked on a park bench in the winter snow. An absolutely gut-wrenching story as she told it and my heart sank for her. Because of Jennifer's history of not feeling loved at home and learning to be invisible to survive high school, she decided to pull up her pants and forge through the rest of the semester keeping, as she called it, her "dirty little secret" to herself. She eventually dropped out of university, never married and worked in a small bookstore back in her hometown. Jennifer's story stained her life.

The next person to share their story was Benite, a radiant, dark chocolate skinned Rwandan refuge camp survivor. At the age of seven, Benite was forced to watch as her father was murdered right in front of her whole family and spent a year living in a tent community, eating rations and lining up daily for water. When she emigrated with her mother and younger sister to Canada the whole of their possessions fit into one suitcase. Benite had to learn a new culture and a new language, in a new colder climate, while dealing with the horrors she had seen in Rwanda replay in her mind at night while she tried to sleep. And yet, she worked hard, studied harder, graduated from law school, and today is the director of an esteemed non-profit. Benite's story served her life.

There were few dry eyes in the room after Benite share her inspirational story, but Jennifer sat inconsolable in a puddle of tears. The workshop leader spent the rest of the morning focused on Jennifer and her inability to deal with the unfairness of her own traumatic life as it resurfaced again and again while two more people shared their stories.

I decided not to return to the workshop after lunch and instead took a walk in the woods. I found a place to sit down with my journal and wrote out what I would have shared with the group. I sat with my memories and I cried for the innocent little girl inside of me who was forced to grow up too fast. I wrote and wrote until my hand cramped and brought myself all the way to the present day. The sun peeked though the branches and the red and orange leaves at a much lower angle, telling me that I needed to head back to the centre soon. But I had one more question to be answered. How was I going to use these stories from my life to help me the way Benite's stories helped her, and to not have me owning the "victim role" the way Jennifer did?

As I asked myself the question, a chickadee landed on my notebook and just as quickly flew away, causing enough of a breeze to turn the page to a blank one. I took this as a sign from the Universe. I needed to turn the page on my life and write the ending to the story as I want it to be and not as a reflection of how the last chapter had been.

I don't share this to minimize the trauma Jennifer endured. Far from it. There are no small traumas. It's not that we were slighted or violated that matters, it's how we feel at that moment that defines the experience for us. There should never be one-upmanship between people who have been hurt in the past as it only extends feelings of victimization. The comparison doesn't lie in how hurt each person was, but in what they did with the rest of their lives after they were hurt.

People who know of my childhood sexual abuse often tell me how strong I am and ask how it is possible to be so resilient. I believe that my strength comes from learning to stand on my story to propel me forward. This is what I've learned from processing my own trauma stories and those of the many women I have worked with in my career.

To heal from our stories, we first must **Stand In** them. We need to face them head on with our hearts open, sink into their truths, write them out in black and white, cry the cleansing tears, get angry, and laugh out loud. We need to feel safe to stand in our trauma and stay there. Very often this is done in therapy or with an individual who is well-trained and implicitly trusted.

Then we need to **Stand Beside** our stories. Continue to hold on to what the stories mean to us and our life but from a slight distance, allowing some space to come between our experiences to allow for an interpretation of what the stories represent. This is the thinking with our head exercise.

And then we need to **Stand Above** our stories. Become the observer by having a wide-angled meta view. What did the other players believe and feel? Not excusing, but explaining what could possibly have been going on outside of what happened directly to us. This is where our feelings and thinking and ego are gone from our stories and it's our higher selves, souls or spirits that are looking at the situation from afar.

And then we need to **Stand On** our stories. Use them for the lessons and blessings they have afforded us. How do we see life differently? What will we never do again? What will we always do from this day forward? Let *how* we behave in the world as a result of what we've learned and lived through, be our calling card and badge of honour more so than having our scars define us.

And finally, we need to **Move On** from our stories. Don't let our past be a dark stain on our hearts and a dark cloud hanging over our heads. The best way to do this, as I have learned from all trauma survivors I have seen thrive in the world, is to take responsibility for our wellbeing and mental health, do the work to heal, and then focus on helping others.

Moving my attention from what's been done to me to what I can do for others is the secret to freedom from my past. It was the secret to Benite's success as well. There are thousands of stories of people who have moved on from horrible adversity to lead fulfilling, purpose driven lives. Look for those stories and may they be an inspiration for you to do your good work in the world too.

ABOUT TAMMY PLUNKETT

Tammy Plunkett left her career as a registered nurse to stay home and raise her four children. She eventually got bored watching Sesame Street and returned to her first love — writing. Tammy spent a few years working solely in fiction and then switched gears. Her studies of psychology and spirituality lead to a desire to inspire others through her talks, her blog on Huffington Post and her first book, *Being Human: Inspiration for Balancing Mind Body and Spirit.* As a Certified Professional Co-Active Coach, she empowers women to connect to their stories and use them to fuel their writing, their business, and their lives. Most recently, Tammy founded Big Sky Author Services where she and her team help launch successful author careers, taking them from an idea to holding their book to selling numerous copies, ensuring that the messages of inspiration are shared widely and make a difference in readers' lives.

www.TammyPlunkett.com
www.bigskyauthorservices.com
www.facebook.com/TammyPlunkettAuthor
www.facebook.com/BigSkyAuthorServices

Acknowledgments

*T*HIS BOOK WOULD not have been possible without the generous and vulnerable sharing of the stories by my 29 co-authors. I would also like to thank Tammy Plunkett and the Big Sky Author Services team who taught me to believe in myself, and that I can write. Tammy encouraged and inspired me to use my storytelling skills and translate them onto paper. She was amazing and I love her for everything she did on this project. Huge thanks to David Moratto's artistic vision for the book cover and interior design. He took an idea in my mind and made it real. For the production magic and editing giftedness, I am very grateful for Dawn James and Christine Bode.

I would love to thank Monique MacDonald for sparking my journey into spirituality and connecting with other women on a different level. She was instrumental in showing me my Sacred Gifts and how to use them to help others be all they can be. For their eternal support and adoration, Sue, Alexandra and Luke. My mom always told me as a child that impossible doesn't exist and what we want to do we can do. Merci, Maman!

About The Cover Art & Artist

❦

The art work is called *Spirit Woman — Talking Stick*
This Ceremonial Earth Goddess sculpture embodies Women Talk.
Spirit Woman — Talking Stick is made from driftwood, shells, four
quartz crystals, and feathers. The sculpture was inspired by the soft
wind bringing breath and by the elements of nature.

DRIFTWOOD: while each tree celebrates its own unique magical
qualities, when wood becomes enveloped in water's ebb and flow, its original
properties and form become altered by the additions of other
multiple energies it then encounters. The wood absorbs the new energies
from life sources which are also housed within the water. And too,
since it no longer is restrained by roots and earth, within its newfound
freedom of travel, wood's magical energy base and form is then continuously
enhanced by a multitude of natural forces.

QUARTZ CRYSTAL: is a power stone. It enhances energy by absorbing,
storing, amplifying, balancing, focusing, and transmitting. It channels
universal energy. Quartz also enhances thoughts, as they are a form of
energy. Because it directs and amplifies energy, it is extremely beneficial
for manifesting, healing, meditation, protection, and channeling. Quartz
is a stone of clarity which dispels and clears away negative energy. It can
be used to purify and clarify on the spiritual, mental, and physical planes.
It is powerfully protective because of these properties. Quartz enhances
spiritual growth, spirituality, and wisdom. Because it clarifies thought
processes and emotions, it can increase inspiration and creativity. It can
also help particularly with concentration, studying, and retaining what
one learns. Quartz is also a stone of harmony because it balances energies,
and is even helpful in romantic relationships.

FEATHERS: the symbolic meaning of feathers deals with ascension and spiritual evolution to a higher plane.

SEASHELLS: they connect us to the ocean and to water energy. Water is the element that represents our emotions. By being in contact with seashells, we open and activate our intuition and sensitivity. This allows us to be able express our imagination, and our creativity.

When we are able to express and share our emotions and ideas, we begin to heal ourselves and have a greater impact on others and the healing of our planetary family.

DEBRA BERNIER grew up as the middle child in a home without TV and was free to wander and explore her world, encouraged by her mother to befriend squirrels, bring home salamanders, unearth bones, and cherish bird's nests. One of Debra's earliest memories is digging at the beach, discovering the rich, dark clay layered under the sand. Buckets of clay were hauled home and soon the family's spider-webbed shed was converted into Debra's childhood studio. Clay figures of animals and mermaids would be sculpted, only to dry out and crumble. Never one to be discouraged, she soon found new mediums to work with and would later complete a B.Ed at Ottawa University, Canada.

Today, Debra still collects shells and stones, and with her husband, encourages her two beautiful, messy children to explore nature's diversity. Living on Vancouver Island means Debra has an endless supply of driftwood to work with; her favorite medium. Like the bones of past trees, each piece of driftwood holds a story and the spirit of nature. Debra hopes that her art inspires creativity and awakens a connection to the beauty of nature.

www.debrabernier.com
www.facebook.com/shapingspirit
www.shapingspirit.etsy.com

Connect with Women Talk

*Women Talk is ordinary women
sharing their extraordinary stories.
By sharing their stories, women make
their communities stronger.*

HOW TO CONNECT WITH WOMEN TALK

Go to womentalk.ca today for a listing
of all our locations across the country.

SIGN-UP TO:

- *Be a Guest*
- *Be a TALKer (in person or virtually)*
- *Be a Sponsor*
- *Be a Volunteer*
- *Be a Chapter Director*

*For more information about booking Brigitte Lessard-Deyell
as a motivational speaker, contact:*
brigitte@womentalk.ca